Ithaca

Ithaca

Alie Benge

TE HERENGA WAKA
UNIVERSITY PRESS

Te Herenga Waka University Press
Victoria University of Wellington
PO Box 600, Wellington
New Zealand
teherengawakapress.co.nz

A catalogue record is available at the National Library of New Zealand.

ISBN 978-1-77692-076-1

The writing and publication of this book were generously supported by

Printed in Singapore by Markono Print Media Pte Ltd

Place me like a seal over your heart,
like a seal on your arm;
for love is as strong as death.

For David of course

Contents

The new Jerusalem

'Are you watching?'

Mum nodded, hovering near the door.

'Come closer,' ordered Theresa. 'You'll have to do this yourself when I'm gone.'

I sat on the kitchen bench next to the pot of boiling water. A blister had formed at the edge of my big toenail and was starting to turn the nail black. Theresa gripped my foot in her hand, pulling it close to her body as I kicked.

'Do you want your foot to fall off, Alie?'

I shook my head.

'Then hold still.'

With a pair of tongs, she pulled the scalpel from the boiling water, touching the sharp edge against the corner of my toenail. 'Come on, stop all this whining. This will teach you to wear shoes outside. You're not in New Zealand anymore.' Pressing down, she slid the scalpel along the toenail and something white exploded from the cut, puffing out as she squeezed the toe. I huffed angry tears, and hiccupped, but the pressure under my toenail, which had been building for weeks, immediately released.

'Hah, cool!' said Mum.

Theresa plucked tweezers from the pot of water, digging them under the white stuff, prising it out and wiping it onto a cloth.

Turning to Mum, she said, 'The jiggers are mites, and this white stuff is their larvae. We're lucky this was caught before they hatched or the foot could have turned gangrenous. Make sure the girls wear shoes every time they go outside. Every time. Closed shoes. Check everyone's toes regularly.' Mum nodded, wide eyed. 'Now, you can go back to your other kids. I'll finish disinfecting this and send her home when it's done.'

I sat with my foot in a bowl of hot water and Dettol, watching baboons sitting on the dirt road, scratching themselves. In the distance, the Ethiopian mountains were starting to disappear in the afternoon rains.

Find the beginning

I wasn't there, but I can see the scene clearly enough, and I don't need to be told what the preacher was like. I know enough of preachers. I'm sure he knew which parts of scripture to recite, which parts to leave out. I bet he was wearing an oversized suit jacket and round glasses. Maybe he hitched up his pants and rocked on his heels as he spoke about the war in Ethiopia, the famine, the need for schools and water projects. When he neared the end, he would have rushed his words together, leaned forward and raised his arms. At the end of his speech he said, 'Who today has heard the call? Who will go?'

My parents looked at each other. They'd never spoken about this before, but they rose from their seats.

'We'll go.'

We have a photo that was taken at the airport. All of us in a row. Two sets of grandparents. Grandma is carrying Dijana. She has her hand on Mum's arm, like maybe she could stop her leaving. My parents have roses in their cheeks. They're the youngest they've ever been.

When I see the photo I remember my nose against the glass, asking Dad how planes work, how a thing so big and heavy, with all of us in it, was supposed to float in the air. I recognised the planes from the ad on TV, with the birds that flew into the shape of a koru and 'Pōkarekare Ana' playing.

I imagine I would have stopped listening as soon as Dad said, 'curvature of the wing', or 'downward force'. He's never been one to dumb things down. That he knew the answer was enough. I got on the plane because he did.

Mum remembers landing in Ethiopia at night, driving through Addis Ababa, unable to make out anything but a few small lights. Years later, she'd say, 'Why did we arrange to land at midnight?' and Dad answered, 'We didn't. We landed in the afternoon. Don't you remember? Someone from the agency picked us up in the van and Carol the Cultural Immersion Guru sent us to Merkato, and you got spat on, and then the taxi crashed. I remember thinking *What have I done? Why have I brought us here?'*

The memory righted itself in Mum's mind. It shook off its dark cloak. But still, even though she knows it was daylight, all her memories from that first week take place during the night. Shopping, going to language school, eating lunch – all of us shuffling around in the dark.

2016, Lesley

'Let's talk about Ethiopia,' said Lesley. She capped the marker she'd used to write my whole life on the whiteboard. I wanted to drink my water but I'd have to lean forward and my chair squeaked when I moved.

'How old were you?'

I hadn't expected Ethiopia to come up. It wasn't what I came here to talk about. I wanted to know why I feel anxious about making dinner, or finding a carpark, certain types of lighting, or being left suddenly alone.

'I was three when we arrived and six when we left.'

'They're very formative years.'

'I guess so.'

'What do you remember?'

'Not much. We were sent to Shishinda – an isolated village. It isn't even on the maps. I miss it sometimes. A lot of the time, actually.'

Lesley flicked her head to get her fringe out of her eyes.

'It must have been lonely. Being removed from your own culture at that age is difficult. Did you have friends? Pets?'

'One friend, but she didn't speak English and I didn't speak Kafa. We had a lot of pets. A goat named Andy, and two rabbits, Sophie and Noah.'

'They're strange names for animals.'

'I named them after the kids I'd known in Addis. Other missionary kids.'

'And what happened to them?'

'To the animals? We ate them.'

At our next session, she pulled out a manilla folder of printed articles and flicked through them. 'I've been doing some reading about missionary kids,' she said. 'You fit under the umbrella of third-culture kids. Basically, any big move at a young age is traumatic, even changing schools. People who moved a lot as children seem to develop issues with sustaining long-term relationships, they rarely feel tied to a place – like there's nothing to hold them down. They struggle to find a sense of belonging. Does any of this ring a bell for you?'

'Are you meant to tell patients this stuff?' I asked. 'Won't I start changing my symptoms to match your description?'

'I prefer the term "clients". And you haven't told me many symptoms.'

'There are no symptoms to tell – not from Ethiopia.'

'Okay, here's a theory. Now it's just an idea and we can try it on for size. It seems that your anxiety is triggered by uncertainty. You say you fill gaps where you see them, that you feel it's your responsibility to fix things no one else is fixing. I have to wonder if this comes from being so young and recognising uncertainty in your parents. Your parents couldn't fix things, so you tried to become the fixer.' She sat back in her chair, her fingers folding together over the stack of articles. 'This must have affected you. At that age you want to feel that your parents can look after you.'

'They did the best they could.'

'I'm sure they did. But still . . .'

I reached for the water, my chair squeaking. I sipped it to fill the silence.

'Tell me, Alie. How many times have you moved – house, city, country – as an adult?'

'Since leaving home? Maybe fifteen, twenty.'

'In how many years?'

'Ten.'

'Right.'

We stared at each other across the marked coffee table and the box of tissues she routinely pushed towards me.

'I'm sorry to disappoint you, Lesley, but I had a happy childhood. I ran around outside. I rewatched *Anne of Green Gables* because it was the only video we had. Maybe I couldn't speak to other kids in Shishinda, but I

16

had my family. I think we're barking up the wrong tree here.'

'And when you came back to New Zealand, what was that like?'

'I don't remember coming back.'

'Leaving Ethiopia?'

'No, those memories are gone.'

'But you were six years old by that point and it was a significant event. You should be able to remember. I think that's what I'm trying to get at. You should remember, but you don't. Something's gone wrong.'

Shishinda

After living in Addis for a year, Dad was sent to Shishinda early to meet the missionary family we'd be replacing. The family in Shishinda had a son my age, so Dad took me with him. The family needed to leave quickly. The wife wasn't well. The loneliness of the place had become too much. It had gotten inside her and hollowed her out.

Dad had taken to filming everything and sending it back to New Zealand so our grandparents could see us grow up. Years later, I watch the footage on my laptop. It's static at first, then the screen flickers and I'm trotting down the runway, Velcro sandals slapping. I'm clutching the straps of my green backpack. I remember something of this flight, how peaceful it had been that high up, despite the noise of the helicopter rotors and the voices in the earmuffs. The people on the ground had shrunk and disappeared, then the cars, then it was like looking at a Lego town, like I could scoop it all back into a box.

Dad's voice narrates in the background of the film. When the city thins out and gives way to patchwork pastures and low mountains, the shadow of the helicopter can be seen on the ground below. Now the houses are round and thatched, smoke lifting through the roofs. Now it's bright green, and from behind the laptop I start to recognise the features, there's a familiar bend in the road, and there's our house at the foot of a mountain, a vast green meadow stretching out before it. Behind it, the huge tree we hung a tyre swing in, not realising it was worshipped by the local people. The helicopter starts to circle down and the camera clicks off.

Everyone must have heard the helicopter coming and rushed towards the house, because when the footage starts again, there's a crowd of at least a hundred Ethiopians, including a wiry man with a deeply lined face and an AK-47 slung over his shoulder. He's talking to a white man wearing beige cargo pants. From out of shot, a woman's voice is explaining to Dad that he needs to bring plenty of blankets because it gets so cold, and that there will be thick fog every morning, rain most nights. There's me with a blond boy, trying to pick up the pigeons that have landed in front of the house.

In the next shot, Dad is walking up to a round hut explaining to the camera that this is the local church. A group of baboons watch suspiciously in the background, looking back over their shoulders. Then Dad is inside the church and it's full of people sitting on the ground staring into the camera, silently. When the shot changes, the same people are clapping and singing. Some have their eyes closed, their heads tipped back. Someone is ululating.

Two years later we were also leaving in a hurry. Nanna and Poppa had come to Shishinda to help us pack up. I'd shown Poppa the jungle gym Dad built and the ladder he could climb to reach the top of the slide. I'd run ahead of him down to the chicken coop and explained that there were no chickens left because there was a leopard in the backyard and, between the leopard and the eagles, all the chickens had been eaten. I showed him the rabbit hutch and the empty collar that used to hang around the goat's neck, and explained that those animals had been eaten too, but by us so it was OK. I told him that one time Dad took the bucket of scraps outside to feed our last chicken, just in time to see an eagle swoop down, scoop up the chicken in its claws, and carry it, squawking, over the trees. Dad just turned around and came back inside.

Across the small gully was the cluster of thatched huts where my friend Miserite lived, and while we watched her mother pick stones out of her teff field, I asked Poppa to tell me about New Zealand.

'Well.' He tilted his head back and locked his fingers together. 'There aren't many people. Where I live it can get very windy, but you'll be nice and warm in Tauranga. The beaches there have black sand.'

'I've never seen a beach. Only big lakes like the one at Bishoftu.'

'You have. You've seen lots of beaches, but you don't remember.'

'Are there hyenas at the beach?'

'Hyenas? Why would there be hyenas at the beach?'

'There are hyenas at Bishoftu.'

Poppa dropped his head into his hands. 'No, there are no hyenas at the beach. No jiggers either, so you can walk outside without shoes. And the roads there are black and smooth. We have grocery stores called New World. They're brightly lit and the fruit is stacked in neat piles. The meat is cut up and wrapped so it doesn't look like the animal anymore. And you can drink water straight from the tap.'

'No!'

'Yes. You could drink water that comes out of the shower if you really wanted.'

'Are there leopards, like the one that walks around the house?'

He didn't say anything to that.

Let me tell you the last thing I remember.

We were all squashed into the car, packed between bags and boxes that I could only just see over. Poppa drove and Dad sat in the back. The students had all come out to wave us off. I watched our little house disappear in the dust. I can conjure the image so clearly. I can see where everyone stood. But it's the dust that bothers me.

Shishinda wasn't dusty. It was lush and green.

My next memories are of pink curtains in a Kenyan hospital; a Maasai man, draped in red cloth, handing me a copper bracelet. I remember walking along a path with my head down. I remember waking up in a room by myself and screaming till someone found me. The memories are glimpses, as if I opened my eyes for a moment, held my fingers in the shape of a frame, and said 'Click' before closing them again.

After that is a vast blackness in which several things happened that I don't remember. There would have been a flight, of course. My parents tell me they walked through the bread aisle at New World, overwhelmed by choices. They tell me I met my other grandparents and didn't recognise them.

When the memories cut back in, I'm standing in front of a classroom. An adult is holding my hand and a teacher is saying, 'Everyone, say hello to Alie. She's just moved here from Ethiopia and I'm sure we'll have plenty of questions to ask her at morning tea.' Twenty little white faces look at me. They smell like playdough. The teacher twirls a globe. She shows everyone where Ethiopia is and I wish she'd show me New Zealand. I walk from school to our new house counting my steps, repeating words, phrases – creating rituals and repetitions. Something in that vast blackness had made me need to do this, but I don't remember.

In Tauranga I got into the habit of telling people that I was born in Ethiopia. I was starting to realise that having something different about you made you special, and made people want to ask you questions and play with you at lunchtime.

One day, there was a surprise party held at our church. To keep the kids entertained, the adults had organised a game. We sat in the middle of the room while our parents sat on the plastic seats that had been arranged around the perimeter of the room. They cheered us on, laughing at the things we said. The adult leading the game was an old man with a big bushy Santa beard. He would ask questions like, who is the oldest, and the oldest would get a candy cane. Who has the most siblings, who lives closest to the church building; then he asked who was born the furthest away? A few people shouted their birth places: 'Dunedin', 'Australia', 'England'. I stood up, sure this was my chance for a candy cane. I yelled confidently, 'Ethiopia' and stepped forward to receive my prize, but he handed it to the English girl. 'You weren't born in Ethiopia,' he said. 'You just came from there. You were born in Auckland.'

I sat back down, confused by this shift in my identity. I was embarrassed to have acted so confidently in front of everyone but been so wrong. I didn't want to play anymore and sulked by the seats where Mum was sitting with Jo, who was fast asleep on her lap. I absorbed the new information and adjusted what I told people. I started saying I was from Ethiopia. I said this often enough that Mum sat me down and explained that I wasn't from there. I was from here. But I didn't know this place. Here, people had grown up with *Sesame Street* and *Captain Planet*, and I was just watching my first episodes. In assembly, I mouthed the words to the national anthem.

1998

We lived in Tauranga for four years. Mum started work as a bookkeeper. Dad was the stay-at-home parent for Jo until she started school, then retrained as a teacher, but at the time, jobs for teachers were thin on the ground.

I was in my room, carefully peeling stickers off their backing and placing them in my sticker book, when the phone rang. A few minutes later, Dijana burst into my room and announced that Dad had got a job in Australia. She ran around the house saying, 'We're going to Australia! We're going to Australia!' On some iteration of this, she seemed to realise that we were going to Australia, and when I came out of my room, she was crying in the hallway.

My best friend Stephanie had just moved to a new house a bike ride away, which meant my life was perfect. We were going to be in a band called Best Friends Forever and we were intensely focused on our musical ambitions. We would spend afternoons on my trampoline, under the plum tree, or lying on the grass in her backyard, writing down song titles in our band book. At Girl Guides I had a friend who looked so much like me that we could swap name tags and trick the leaders. The kids on my street had formed a gang and we'd ride our bikes around and see who would get closest to the scary house at the end of the street that was clearly haunted. I was nine years old. I didn't want to leave. Not again.

I walked into Mum and Dad's room, trying to keep my face from scrunching, but as soon as I saw them I crumpled, lowered my face onto their bed and asked if we could just stay. Over the next few days, I tried to convince Mum that Australia would be terrible because there were snakes and tarantulas, and they might not have *Coronation Street*. I asked if I could live with Stephanie. I tried everything. One night, inspiration struck. I ran inside to find my parents. 'I've got it,' I said. 'Let's go back to Ethiopia.' By this point, my memories had probably already started shifting, the reality of isolation in Shishinda being replaced by the idyllic images in the home movies. I remembered only that I'd been happy there, that it was my home once and I missed it, and if it was absolutely necessary that we move, maybe we could go back to an old place, instead of forward to a new one.

Mum was silent. Dad said that was enough now.

I cried on the phone to Stephanie and we made a plan to keep our band alive across countries. My bike gang all agreed that we'd write to each other forever, every day, until I was old enough to come back.

That first summer in Queensland was so hot the

house seemed to swell. We spent so long in front of the pedestal fan that my sisters and I made a game of speaking into it as the blades cut our voices into pieces.

We visited Nanna and Poppa in Wellington once, but it was too expensive to fly all of us so each set of grandparents would visit once a year. Eventually even this stopped and I grew up feeling that I didn't know my grandparents. I learned that, when the neighbours mowed their long grass, snakes would come into the house. I learned to check my shoes for spiders, and to stomp loudly when walking in the dark to scare off cane toads. New Zealand took on that hazy memory glow that surrounded the places I'd left.

Nostalgia doesn't seem cognitive. I can't express it in language. It's in the stomach. It's a deep sigh. It grips around my heart when I see the colours that remind me, the smells and sounds. I imagine the colours of Shishinda like a box of colouring pencils, or labels on bottles of nail polish. There's the fuzzed blue of enormous mountains in the distance, the purple of a storm coming, the murky-white of waking to a thick wall of fog, the angry blistered pink of a baboon's arse. The most vivid of all is the green. How do I describe the green of Shishinda? When I think of the place, when I watch the home movies that have been transferred over the years from cassette to VHS to DVD to computer file, it's the green that stands out most. Shishinda green. The green that comes from nine months of rain a year. Shishinda green gives off its own light. It fills the horizon. It rises up to meet you and presses in at the windows. It can be growing dark above but still green below.

When I see a landscape that almost looks like Shishinda, when I hear roosters crowing, or when I'm buried in fog, there it is, that heart-pull, like the feeling after someone has died and you know they're gone but if you could just see them one more time; if you could just—

An idea that wouldn't leave

Returning wasn't a thought I ever consciously settled on. It was an assumption, if anything, that one day I'd go back. I held the two thoughts together, both loosely: the first, that I would be back there one day; the second, that it would never happen. When is a good time to return to your childhood? I'd wondered what it would be like, though, stepping off the helicopter in Shishinda, the grass blown back by the propellers. Our house would be there, waiting for me, and I'd be, I don't know – home?

In a café with my sister Dijana I told her my plan. She paused, coffee halfway to her mouth.

'By yourself?'

'We could all go. I think it would be good for us.' I slid the little napkin out from under my coffee and started shredding it into little pieces. 'We could close the circle. I don't know. Go back to the beginning. Don't you want to see where you grew up?'

'We hardly grew up there. I barely remember it.'

'You must remember something.'

'I remember moments, just glimpses. But I don't know how many are real, or how many I created from photos, or watching Dad's home movies.'

'Glimpses of what?'

'Random things. I remember being carried out of the house when I was sick, all those kids shaking the car, patting the goat, a girl stepping on a nail.'

'That was me! I stepped on the nail,' I laughed.

'Was it? I thought it was one of the other missionary kids. Anyway, that trip sounds like zero fun. Let me know when you want to go to Turks and Caicos.'

I put the idea to Dad as we were hoisting a piece of gypsum board onto what would be the ceiling of their new house. I held the board up while Dad knocked nails in, stopping to swear at the nail gun each time it jammed.

'When are you thinking?' he asked, when it was in place.

'Maybe July.'

We dragged the next piece over.

'Yeah, OK.'

I'd expected more resistance.

'Jo will want to come too. She'll get FOMO,' he added.

Surprisingly, he was right. Jo agreed to come, saying, 'Now I'll be able to scratch it off my scratch map.'

'You haven't scratched off Ethiopia? You were born there.'

'Yeah, but I haven't, like, *been* there. All I have to show for it is a birth certificate no one can read.'

Mum agreed to come but didn't last ten minutes before backing out. So, it was decided. None of us knew what to expect, nor were we particularly looking forward to it. We'd go to Addis, then head north. The traditional tourist route followed the ancient kingdoms: Bahir Dar, Gondar, Axum, and Lalibela. Dad shook his head when I asked how we'd get to Shishinda. 'It's too far. Too isolated. We'd have to hire a helicopter, and if we got stranded there, well.'

Everyone I spoke to – the travel agent, the nurse who immunised me, the woman at the bureau de change – said the same thing: 'Ethiopia? Why are you going there?' I felt like I was saying at every turn, 'I used to live there and now I'm going back. I used to live there. I'm going back.'

The week of the flight I channelled my anxiety into the acquisition of sleeping pills. I couldn't get a doctor's appointment until the day of the flight and I lay awake the night before, running over the plan: go to the doctor, pick up the prescription, pick up Dad, swap cars, pick up Jo, pick up Mum from work so she can leave us at the airport and take the car back. But what if the bags don't fit in the car? What if when we swap the car, I forget to take my suitcase out? What if I get to the airport and realise I don't have my passport? What if the doctor won't give me the prescription? I only needed the pills for the long flights, but I'd made the problem so exaggerated that it bloated in my mind, and my stomach lurched at the thought of not getting them. I sat in the doctor's office, flicking through a magazine, not looking at the pages, checking my watch as each person in front of me took longer than their allotted fifteen minutes. I asked the nurses how long it would be because I had a flight to catch. They said, 'I'm sure it won't be much longer', and, 'Where are you off to?'

'Ethiopia.'

'Ethiopia? Why are you going there?'

A kid screamed and bashed a big plastic truck against the chair legs. After forty minutes I realised I'd have to give it up, and then the doctor finally called my name. She tried to convince me I needed antidepressants instead of sleeping pills, and after ten minutes of trying to convince me I was depressed, I could see why the appointments ran over. I finally wrangled a prescription out of her, ran to the pharmacy, then to the car, clutching the pills to my chest, and raced to pick up Dad and Jo. The drive to the airport was quiet.

At Wellington Airport we sat at a wobbly table under the giant eagle. Jo looked up Ethiopia on Safe Travel, something I was supposed to have done weeks ago. A red warning flashed: 'Extreme Risk!' The site strongly advised against travel to this region. There was political unrest and tourists had been kidnapped. In the past three years, Ethiopia had declared a state of emergency twice. Activists and journalists were in prison, protestors were frequently killed. Tourism had dried up. The warning advised staying away from large groups as they often turned into violent riots. Dad dismissed the warning with a wave of his hand. 'She'll be right. It's too late now.'

I walked through security, flicking my boarding pass nervously against my leg, and heard the guard call me back. I thought I was in trouble, but I'd left my bag, belt, and earrings in the tray after being scanned. I giggled and slapped the side of my head, 'Duh.'

'Jetlag?' asked the guard.

'Sure.'

It was a twelve-hour flight to Hong Kong first. The sleeping pill kicked in after half an hour and I missed most of the flight, waking at the end with my neck frozen on an angle. We had a five-hour layover so we caught the airport train into Kowloon and trudged through a market in the unbearable heat, past rows of stalls, all selling the same phone cases, while my hair frizzed higher and higher in the humidity. We eventually melted back to the airport, only to find the flight to Addis was overbooked. The only people getting on the plane were those with connecting flights, and angry people who slammed their palms on the counter. I tried to muster some aggression but couldn't find it within me. All I could manage was a deep sigh and an eye roll, which I immediately wanted to apologise for. The airline booked us a hotel back in Kowloon, and as we waited for them to extract our bags I watched the Australian couple who'd been behind us in the line. They pointed their fingers, slammed their hands down, and then crossed their arms and refused to leave the line until they were offered a seat on the plane.

The taxi driver sped along the highway, through tunnels and around tight bends, at 200 kilometres an hour. Somehow, after accepting this was how my life would end, we made it to the hotel and I climbed out of the taxi, legs shaking. In the room, I threw my bag in the corner, kicked off my sweaty shoes, and tipped face-forward onto the mattress, which turned out to be hard as stone. I might as well have landed on the floor. I rolled over, eyes watering from the collision of my nose on the mattress, and fell asleep in my clothes.

By 8pm the next day, we were back at the airport. We'd left New Zealand two days ago and we were only halfway to Ethiopia. At the gate, Jo slept on the hard seat next to me, Dad held a book open with his eyes closed. I was too tired to focus my eyes on anything. Our Ethiopian air hostesses flocked towards us, their little suitcases clicking across the tiles. They chatted like birds and I wanted them to recognise me, include me. I wanted to walk over to them and say, 'This country means something to me too.' I wondered what it would be like to find yourself in others, to have a group to belong to, some country that was your own.

We squished into our seats on the plane. The meals were inedible so I broke off enough bread to wrap my sleeping pill, and stayed awake long enough to see the air hostesses had changed from their green suits into traditional dresses and shammas. My head fell forward and I tipped into a broken, cramped sleep.

Landing in Addis felt circular, as if I was in a three-act play. A woman went on a journey / a stranger came to town. I was moving towards an ending in which everything would be tied up neatly. The plot would move back to the beginning. The woman returns to the place she started but has come back changed. I hunched over to look out the window at a view I'd last seen twenty-one years ago.

When I was a child here, people would pull my hair and pinch my skin. Now, as we joined a noisy queue to get our passports stamped, only a few turned to stare.

As I finally hauled my bag off the carousel, after waiting an hour for it to appear, another hand closed around the handle. I clutched tighter, grabbing with both hands, but the man yanked it towards a trolley.

'Oh, thank you,' I said, 'but it's really fine. I can carry it.' He waved his hand, kept tugging, and reached for Jo's bag with the other hand. She yanked it back, but Dad said, 'It's all right. Let him take it.' He loaded his own bag onto the trolley and the man smiled broadly and pushed it behind us as we took off our belts and shoes and passed through security.

The airport was new, and the walls of the arrivals area were lined with bamboo scaffolding. As we passed through the doors, we were immediately surrounded by people waving signs for their hotels.

'Obama Hotel, Miss. Best in town.'

'Sir, we have a swimming pool, Sir.'

'Makeda Guest House. Free shuttle. Great location.'

We pushed through the group, putting our heads down and avoiding eye contact. A uniformed woman gestured for us to follow her outside and we stepped into the smoke and sourdough smell of Addis Ababa. Dad paid the man with our bags after he'd squashed them as far as possible into the boot of a tiny taxi. The woman asked Dad where he wanted to go and when Dad answered in Amharic, both the woman and the driver stepped back and said, 'Gobez, gobez!' The driver introduced himself as Elias, and the three of them bent over the printout from our hotel. With our suitcases still sticking halfway out of the boot, we took off. A photo was clipped onto the air vent in the car. Judging from the clothes and the fact that the man seemed to be posing in a throne room, I assumed he was the Prime Minister, but Elias passed the photo to the backseat without being prompted, and told us it was Teddy Afro, the singer of the bouncy, jangling music he was playing.

'You will hear a lot of him while you are here. All Ethiopia loves him,' said Elias, shaking his shoulders to the music.

Addis Ababa

Driving through the city, Dad chatted in Amharic, slipping into English when he couldn't think of the right word, occasionally leaning back to translate. He said how much everything had changed, how many tall buildings there were now, how many more people. I'd never heard Dad talk so much. To see outside, I had to peer through the gaps between stickers of Tewodros and Haile Selassie that were plastered all over the taxi windows.

Along the road, boys were going car to car selling phone chargers. Men were shovelling gravel onto the back of a truck. Women crouched on the footpath, fanning small fires, roasting corn and coffee, and everywhere, everything was moving. Everyone was in migration.

Elias stopped the car and beckoned to one of the boys in the road. The boy held a plastic tray hoisted on straps slung over his shoulders. Ordered in neat rows on the tray were packets of gum, cards for loading phone credit, and boxes of cigarettes. Elias bought one of the cards and the boy leaned in through the window and said 'Hello ferenji', using the word for 'foreigner'. Elias handed money through the window and said, 'They're not ferenji.'

I wanted to ask Elias to turn around, to take us back. I didn't recognise this place. Jo said quietly, 'I've just realised,

you're the same age Mum was when we arrived last time.'
Elias drove further away from town, away from the built-up area and towards a street of shanty shops and souks. He turned off the road and bumped along a dirt track in an alleyway, past men selling khat out of wheelbarrows, and stopped outside a corrugated-iron fence. I said, 'Are you sure this is the right place?' Outside the hotel gates, the men with wheelbarrows yelled, 'American, hello!' Dad said, 'Sorry girls. It looked different in the photos.'

A cross-eyed man swung the gate open and closed behind us. It was starting to rain and he trotted along, holding an umbrella over Dad's head until we reached the office. The manager, a woman named Mariam, gave us our keys and pointed to the hotel restaurant: Eggy Yummy Diner. The cross-eyed man waited outside to drag our bags up the stairs. I told him it was OK, I could take my own bag, but he waved his hands and prised my fingers off the handle.

In our room I collapsed into a chair. Jo's feet were so swollen from the flight that her usually loose anklet was cutting into her skin. She stumbled towards the bed and lay on it, face down.

From the veranda outside our room, I looked over the city. The early-morning sun was shining through the pollution haze, casting rust-coloured light over Addis. Mount Entoto was fading to purple in the distance. A rooster crowed; someone bashed a hammer against tin. I recognised nothing. I was surprised by how afraid I was.

Eggy Yummy Diner took so long to bring our food out that we took the waiting in shifts. One of us waited in the restaurant while the other two organised themselves for the day ahead, then we'd swap. During my turn to wait, I watched the only other guests in the hotel: a loud Spanish family in the process of adopting two Gambelan girls. The girls smiled and waved at me every few minutes, laughing behind their hands. One girl had a hand with only three fingers, which curled in on themselves, tightly bunched inside the palm.

While we ate, we worked out our itinerary for the day. By this time, I'd reassured myself that we were just in a different part of the city, and I'd soon see the Ethiopia I'd remembered all my life.

Cars squeezed around each other like people in a crowd, tooting their horns in place of indicating. Pedestrians walked freely on the road, trusting drivers to swerve around them. The same Teddy Afro song played on repeat, and Elias danced in his seat, tapping his fingers against the steering wheel.

Elias came with us to the National Museum. The light was dim, and the fossils were so dark. We squinted at the boxes of broken up prehistoric bones. Lucy stood in a glass case, on a piece of stained wood that looked like a chopping board. She was tiny. Only a metre tall. At rest, her arms would have hung to her knees, but they were pulled into a pose. One foot stepped back, and her huge, heavy-looking head tilted upwards, as though she were backing away from something. I forget that these ancient bodies would have looked more like tiny apes than like us. I'd imagined her like myself, or like Lot's wife, looking over her shoulder as she walked out of the Rift Valley.

I asked the woman at reception where the bathroom was and my heart sank as she pointed outside to a slumped, dark tin shack. There was just enough light in the shack to see the bowl was full, the seat was wet. Jo had come to support me.

'Don't do it, Alie.'

'I have to. It's such a bumpy road, and what if this is the only one we see all day?'

A woman waiting behind me trotted off and returned with a bucket of water which she held out to me. I gaped at it, unsure what I was supposed to do, until she sighed, pushed past me, threw the water in the toilet to flush it, and gestured for me to go in. I tiptoed inside, enclosing myself in the dark cubicle. I nearly cried when I turned the tap to wash my hands and found it spun endlessly, but no water came out. I walked out of the shack, my hands stretched at my side, and found Jo shaking her head.

'I can't believe you did that.'

From that point, I stopped drinking water half an hour before we left our hotel, or until we were half an hour from returning to the hotel. I would be thirsty for the next two and a half weeks.

Elias had gotten bored and waited by his taxi, and when we finally wandered back, he took us to the hospital where Jo was born, driving past the part of the road where she was almost born. We drove through the Piazza, past Haile Selassie's palace, and Ghion Hotel: places I knew I'd been before, but I was sure they didn't look like this. And with my heart dropping, I realised what I'd done: I'd forgotten this place. I'd broken my few memories into spare parts and with those parts I'd made something else, something that wasn't real, and then spent my whole life missing it.

The day before our flight to Bahir Dar, Elias took us for coffee near Merkato, and I stood at the bar drinking a macchiato that was so rich and complex I wondered how I'd ever enjoy New Zealand coffee again. Elias insisted we line up along the bar so he could take photos of us on my phone. I didn't want to do this. I didn't want to look like a stupid white girl, turning everything into a happy snap. I didn't want to be a tourist.

On the way back to the taxi a man held a poster of the times tables, similar to one I had on my wall as a kid. I shook my head at him. 'No thank you. But thank you.' He kept jumping around me with the sign until Elias shut the taxi door after me. The man followed the car, the poster pressed against the window, until we were back on the road.

Swiping through the photos Elias had taken, I saw that every head in the café was turned towards us. I was already dreaming of the day when I'd be able to walk through Wellington and have no one notice me.

Of the people we'd known here in 1991, we could only track down Zelalem. He arrived at Eggy Yummy Diner in a shiny suit and graduation gown. 'I told them I must keep this for one more week. I must get one more photo,' he said.

His face had filled out, and he'd grown a beard, flecked with grey. I'd never seen him in anything other than the work clothes he used to wear. I'd imagined he would still be the twenty-year-old I remembered. Not this man in his early forties. It seems almost rude that the people I've trapped in my memory have moved on with their lives and continued to grow and change.

'You grew so tall,' he said, drawing his hand from the top of my head to his chin, to compare my height with his own. 'You used to be down here,' he moved the hand from his chin to his knee.

'And you were just a baby,' he said to Jo. 'How tall are you now?'

'Six foot,' Jo, who interprets any comment about her height as an insult, answered quietly.

'My goodness. They should have put bricks on your head when you were growing up.' We laughed as though we haven't been hearing this joke all our tall lives.

The afternoon rains had started, but we stood at the window and planned where we would take the photo.

'Do you remember you used to join our Bible studies

on the lawn?' he asked.

I didn't remember, but I'd seen the photos of myself lying on my stomach in the circle while the men leaned on their arms and laughed at the camera.

I said, 'Do you remember pushing me around in the wheelbarrow?'

'How could I forget that? I would say, "Let me stop, I have to go home now," and you would say, "No, more, more!"' He chuckled and stroked his beard. Turning to Dad, he asked, 'Are you going back to Shishinda?'

Dad shook his head. 'It's too far. It isn't possible.'

'Ah yes, I got very sick on the drive.'

'Wait – you've been there?'

'Of course. Who do you think built your house?'

We stood in the light from the window, mouths open, not sure what to ask.

The rain drifted away and Zelalem shouted, 'Now!' We bolted to the poinsettia bush and posed. The owner of the hotel dashed out behind us and skidded to a knee. The sun landed on us for a moment and she clicked away on the point-and-shoot camera as many times as she could until a new sheet of rain swept in and we dashed back into Eggy Yummy Diner. Settling on a table, Zelalem clicked through the photos and said, 'Yes, very good. I am so happy.'

Our coffee arrived and I stared into my cup. Dad said, 'You never told us you built our house.'

'Didn't I?' said Zelalem, stirring several teaspoons of sugar into his tiny coffee. 'Perhaps it never came up. I was arrested there.'

'Wait, what?' Dad leaned forward. Jo and I glanced at each other and put our coffees down.

'I went with the leader of the agency you were with. You never met him. Jacob was his name. We drove down with a big truck full of building materials. We marked out where to dig and put stakes down. We'd barely been going an hour when the kebele showed up. They had a gun and everything. They wanted to know what we were doing. So Jacob said, "We're building a mission station for a school. It's all been arranged." But the kebele said, "It hasn't been arranged with us. This is communal grazing land."'

Dad muttered, 'Well, that explains why we were always having to shoo cows out of the garden.'

Zelalem continued. 'They wanted to arrest Jacob. He was a ferenji of course. But he was old then. I said, "Take me instead," and they did. I sat on the mud floor of an empty room for two days and two nights. I guess they came to an arrangement, because eventually I was let out and we got back to building your house. Jacob started feeling sick while in Shishinda. Shortly after we came back to Addis, he was diagnosed with prostate cancer and went home to America to die. The next family who came, the wife had a mental breakdown. The one after that, the husband got prostate cancer. Then your family, your mum with her illness. The next family, tuberculosis. One more after that. They were kicked out at gunpoint, and then there were no more ferenji in Shishinda.'

We knew all this. A few years after we left Ethiopia, when we were living in Tauranga, a man came to our door. He gave us the same list. He said, 'You were surrounded by witch doctors. Hundreds of them. Thousands. If you're better now, you're the lucky ones.' Not everyone survived Shishinda.

After a few hours, Dad said we needed to go because we had a flight to Bahir Dar, and Zelalem gathered up his gown, said he'd visit us in New Zealand one day, and revealed that his sister had been outside the gate the entire time, waiting to drive him home.

Bahir Dar

We asked a staff member to point us in the direction of our departure gate, but instead he led us to an office and produced three Styrofoam cups, putting a black tea bag and a chai tea bag in each one. The water he poured from the filter was cold and he said, 'Oh, I'm so embarrassed.' So we assured him we preferred it cold until he smiled again, and we stood around his desk, drinking cold, vaguely spicy water.

'It's been a while since I saw a tourist,' he said. 'There are so many problems now. So much fighting. No one wants to come.' He talked for ten minutes, stopping only to take deep breaths. He talked like a man who had shot his head above water and had to get it all out before slipping back under. Eventually we gently interrupted and said we needed to find our gate. 'Of course, of course,' he said. 'I talk too much. My wife always tells me.' He walked us to the gate and before leaving he asked, 'Are you going to Africa while you're here?'

We squinted, unsure how to answer, not wanting to say the wrong thing. Jo asked, 'Aren't we – aren't we in Africa now?'

The man sighed and shook his head. 'No, I mean like *Africa* Africa. This is not really Africa. I mean the black area.' It was easier to say no, we weren't going to Africa.

Lake Tana in Bahir Dar is the source of the Blue Nile. It's so wide that, even from the high balcony of our hotel, I couldn't see the other side. The lake is dotted with islands that poke up through the water, hours apart from each other, many housing ancient monasteries. The hotel clerk told us a tour group would be leaving shortly for the islands, but when we were picked up in a minivan, we found we were the group. This shouldn't have surprised us. I'd only seen a handful of other tourists so far. The minivan dumped us unceremoniously at a tired-looking jetty packed with construction workers. We assumed he was parking the van before giving us directions, but we looked back to see him already disappearing down the road. Turning towards the jetty, we found every face looking at us.

Jo and I hung back, thinking of the Travel Safe warning about tourists being kidnapped, but Dad, fearless or reckless, seemed unfazed by the attention. He ambled calmly to the end of the jetty, hands clasped in front, smiling out at the water, not bothered at all by the fact that we seemed to have been abandoned in an industrial area with no tour in sight.

A woman approached Jo and held up her forearms to display a selection of thin scarves wafting lightly in the breeze off the lake.

'You wanna buy a scarf?'

Jo made a nervous sound and said, 'Oh, no thank you.'

'You sure? Pretty colour?' The woman selected a scarf the colour of blood and held it against Jo's skin. 'What about for your mother?' she asked, lifting a scarf to my own neck. Maybe blue? Nice.'

Jo started laughing.

I said, 'I'm only four years older. Sheesh.'

We backed away from the woman until she gave up and took her scarves elsewhere, and found Dad surrounded by five of the workers, who had taken a break from shovelling gravel into a truck.

'Oh no,' said Jo. 'We're so getting kidnapped.' But then the sound of laughter rang out, and one of the men gestured to us as we got closer.

'Your daughters?' the man asked Dad. 'Which was born here?' Dad pointed to Jo.

'I'll give you . . .' The man put his hand to his chin and leaned back, as though appraising her. 'Five cows.' The men threw their heads back and roared. They shouted their own offers. Dad said, 'Her boyfriend doesn't have any cows, so I'll consider your offer.' This set them off again and they slapped their knees and clutched their stomachs.

Jo cringed and scanned the lake for the boat. I was low-key offended that within a few minutes I'd been mistaken for Jo's mother, and not been exchanged for cows.

The men asked Dad where we'd lived in Ethiopia all those years ago, when the country was holding its breath after a civil war; when we walked past dead bodies in the street and fell asleep to the sound of gunfire.

He said, 'Shishinda', and the men shook their heads.

He said, 'A little village a few hours from Jimma.'

'Ohhh,' said the men. 'The black region.' They asked why he came to this country and he said, 'I was an aid worker.' He always says aid worker. He never says missionary. Because how absurd, how offensive, to come to the oldest Christian nation in the world, a country that was Christian before Rome, as a missionary.

Finally, a boat swept into the jetty and a tall man jumped out, approaching us. He asked if we were the tour group. Dad said goodbye to his new friends and we climbed aboard the small boat, spreading out across the bench seating. The skipper asked where we'd come from, and when Dad said, 'New Zealand', he replied, 'Ah, Amsterdam. I would love to go there.'

'No, New ZEAland. Not the Netherlands. It's near Australia.'

'Ahhh,' said the skipper, tipping his head back. 'I know, I know. Anchor Butter.'

Dad laughed. 'Yes, we make Anchor Butter.'

The skipper answered, 'Many sheep. Good at rugby.'

It took an hour speeding across the water before we reached the nearest island. On the way we passed a boy in a tiny papyrus boat that technically floated, but was mostly submerged under the weight of its passenger. The brown lake water sloshed over the sides and onto his legs. He was soaking wet. People from the monasteries have been rowing back and forth to the mainland on these boats for thousands of years, shipping deliveries of coffee beans grown on the islands, or seeds and other supplies. I asked the skipper how long it would take to cross the lake. 'From the nearer islands, maybe eight hours.'

'And the further ones?'

He shrugged his shoulders. 'About eighteen.'

I tried to imagine being alone for eighteen hours, on a tiny boat, in a vast lake, with fifteen metres of water underneath me, trying to find my way in the dark.

A thin man named Noah met us on the jetty of the first island and began the tour. He spoke in a monotone, waving his arms carelessly towards whatever he was referencing, barely able to conceal his boredom with this routine, which he'd probably performed a thousand times. A crowd of children followed us, gripping flutes, and necklaces made from coins minted with a bust of Haile Selassie. The children raised their handfuls of treasures, shouting prices, and reducing those prices as we trooped around the island.

Noah, with his eyes half closed, knocked a piece of wood against a stone gong and explained that this was how messages were sent to the monks. He half-heartedly flung a finger towards a thatched hut where men were crouched, reading the Bible, pulling their shammas further around their arms. 'This is our Bible college,' he said. 'These monks are learning to write poetry and songs in Ge'ez.'

With a deep sigh he approached a round chapel and spoke quickly, as though trying to be done with us as soon as possible. 'So, twelve panels on the walls to represent the twelve apostles. Seven windows represent the seven miracles that Jesus performed on the cross. On the roof, up there, see the white thing? Ostrich egg. Ostriches never rest or leave their eggs and Jesus never leaves us, so all Ethiopian churches have an ostrich egg stuck on top. OK?'

Jo interrupted, 'If the ostrich never leaves the eggs, how did you take them?'

Noah slid a stink eye in her direction, ignored the question, and returned to his monologue.

'The chapel is built in three concentric circles to represent the Trinity: the Father, the Son, and the Holy Spirit. Each circle is under one roof to make up one structure, just as the members of the Trinity make up one being. In the centre circle is a replica of the Ark of the Covenant. The real one, obviously, is in Axum.'

I thought back to my own Bible college and the lecturer standing behind a podium saying, 'We will never understand the Trinity. It isn't possible for us to comprehend. But maybe it's like steam, ice and water. All different forms of the same thing. But it's also nothing like that because those things aren't in relationship with each other. It's an imperfect metaphor.' He'd then explained that Jesus is God, the Father is God, and the Holy Spirit is God. But God is not Jesus, nor the Holy Spirit. The Son is not the Father. Each is only itself and not the other, but they are one God, and not three Gods. Never three.

I imagined these three circles of the building as a bird might see them, looking straight down. Three sections of one unit. I said to Noah, 'That might be the best explanation of the Trinity I've heard.'

'Yes, well, not everyone can read the Bible. The shape of the church explains the nature of God. The seven windows show his sovereignty while dying. The egg shows how much he loves you.' Noah walked up to the chapel and kissed the wall before entering, touching his forehead to the door post. I wanted to cry with how beautiful it was.

On the way back, the skipper said he wanted to show us something, and turned the boat into an inlet, letting the engine go silent. He sat, peering over the water while we wondered what he was up to, and finally pointed his finger and said, 'There.'

A hippo sat in the water, eyes trained on us. The water rippled behind it, and then, out of the ripples, a baby hippo broke the surface. The hippos and the four of us watched each other, no one moving. The big hippo harrumphed under the water, and the baby dipped below and resurfaced, flicking its ears. After a while, the skipper said, 'I think you are happy,' and we said, 'Yes, very happy.' Later, in a restaurant on the lake, we retold Shishinda stories, as we do. Repeating the same yarns we all know, laughing at the same points, constructing our family mythology. Dad told us again about the chickens. How the leopard in the backyard kept slinking under the wire, disappearing back into the bush with a hen in his mouth, and how birds would come from above to take the little chickens, and how the huge eagle swooped down right in front of him, dodged the protective mesh Dad had put over the pen, and took off with the last of our birds, just as Dad had gone out to feed it. I feel I remember this story, like I was watching from the window as Dad looked down at the bucket of scraps, shrugged his shoulders, and brought the bucket back inside. But maybe I've just been told it so many times. Maybe memory is nothing.

Gondar

It was late in the afternoon when we arrived in Gondar. The hotel restaurant was on a high pavilion, and as we ate injera we watched the light fade over the city. Kids played in the street below us and women sat in groups, watching the children while roasting corn in their braziers or pounding coffee beans.

Now that we were halfway through our trip, I was finally starting to feel comfortable, confident that I wasn't going to be kidnapped or caught in a riot.

A map of Ethiopia was Blu-Tacked to the wall in the hotel lobby, as it was in most of the lobbies. But here, the name 'Shishinda' jumped off the page. It seemed to call me over. I'd never seen Shishinda on a map before. The place is so remote, I could have made it up.

'Shishinda, Shishinda!' I exclaimed. But the only person there was Taye, the hotel manager. He nodded politely.

In the morning, we sat in the pavilion, puffy-eyed, as an Ethiopian Orthodox mass blasted through the air. We'd been woken early in the morning by the sound and as Taye took our order he said, 'It's worse at the church. I have to cover my ears.'

'What about the mosque?' I asked. 'Don't they need to do their call to prayer?'

'They have a schedule,' answered Taye. 'They share the airspace.'

The wi-fi only worked on the roof and I scrolled through Facebook, trying to distract myself from the blaring in my ears.

Our tour guide met us at the hotel and introduced himself as Muhammad, tucking his left palm against his forearm while shaking our hands. He hailed a bajaj and we drove to a compound of medieval castles.

Muhammad led us through ancient spas, and lion pens, and showed us the room where an Ethiopian queen had taught women to defend themselves by throwing berbere spice in their enemies' eyes. One of the stone pavilions had been used as a garage by Italian soldiers, but was once a vast library. In the centre of the compound was a blackened archway, formerly a grand entrance hall until the English bombed it in their efforts to help free Ethiopia from the Italians.

Muhammad pointed to the top of a low wall where huge cylindrical beehives were quietly buzzing.

'It has an interesting smell,' I said. 'Not like honey at all. Kind of funky.'

Muhammad watched Jo, Dad and me as we stood under the hives taking deep breaths through our noses, trying to describe the smell. Finally he said, in his dry monotone, 'You're standing next to the toilet.'

The bottom of the compound was a lush, moss-covered lane where a yellow cow was tied to a tree. Jo and I patted the cow and she looked up at us through her moon eyes and her long lashes and Muhammad explained, 'We have a holy day. Several families buy a cow together. She's waiting to be slaughtered,' then walked away, his phone jangling. Dad said, 'Muhammad doesn't pull any punches.'

Mum had asked us to buy her a cotton gabi on our trip. The ones she had bought twenty-four years ago were almost threadbare. We hadn't been able to find one but Muhammad said he knew someone at the market who made them, so we planned to meet him there after lunch. A crowd of children followed us through the cobbled streets as we looked for somewhere to eat. One of the girls held out her hand to shake Jo's and Jo took it. Immediately the kids swarmed, each holding their hand out to be shaken. Jo's eyes widened as she tried to meet every tiny outstretched hand, but the group grew, children running out of their homes, until she had to tuck her hands under her arms and say, 'Sorry, I'm sorry.' We waded through the crowd of children and ducked under a low doorway into a dark, cave-like restaurant. Dad scanned the menu and started laughing, pointing to two different shiro dishes. 'This one is normal shiro,' he said, 'and this one is called fat person shiro.'

I knew this wouldn't be the kind of market that sold food and phone cases. This would be where people brought their goods to trade. There would be mud, crowds, shivering goats, donkeys carrying huge loads, souks with animal carcasses stretched on a rack – their ribs broken open. But we hadn't yet been kidnapped. We'd crossed the source of the Nile in a rickety boat, we were getting used to being stared at and followed. So I made a conscious decision not to be afraid, and I dove into the crowd.

Jo stuck close behind me as the four of us picked our way through. I heard a cow lowing hysterically and turned to the sound in time to see a burst of blood as its body fell to the ground. *It's fine. It's OK*, I said to myself. *Every time I've been scared, it's turned out OK. This is all good. We're all good.*

We approached a narrow lane between stalls and souks. The previous night's rains had left the path thick with mud. We crossed the mud slowly and I reached the other side first, where a hump of more solid earth jutted out, and wound up and away around a corner. Muhammad and I stood on this small ledge and waited for Dad and Jo. Someone behind me yelled, 'Beautiful, beautiful.' Turning, I saw a tiny man leaning against a souk. His knitted green beanie had a hole in it, and his two front teeth were missing. He clapped his whole palm against his mouth and blew me a kiss. Muhammad said, 'Pretend you can't hear.'

We looked back in time to see Jo's foot slip off a stone and slump deep into the mud. Muhammad jumped down and carefully walked over to her. She put a hand on Dad's shoulder and a hand on Muhammad's, trying to work the foot out of the mud, but it was sunk over her ankle and she'd lose her shoe if she pulled it out. She was trying to wriggle her foot in such a way that she could keep the shoe on, when suddenly Muhammad and Dad leapt closer in together as two donkeys bolted past, almost colliding with them. Jo, startled by the donkeys, yanked her bare foot out.

Suddenly, cold fingers wrapped around me and pulled. The toothless man was tugging my arm, pulling me down to him, his lips puckered. I twisted away, trying to pull my arm out at the weakest point of the grip, where the thumb and fingers joined, but he slapped his other hand around my arm. I stumbled, but rebalanced my feet further apart for a stronger position. I should have rammed my knuckles into his windpipe like I'd been taught, but that felt too violent and I hesitated. It had all happened so quickly. Three, maybe four seconds. Then Muhammad leaped back onto the plateau, slammed his palm into the man's face and prised the fingers off me.

A taller man, with ears sticking out like teacup handles, came racing out of his stall and smacked his hand against the toothless man's head, knocking his beanie off.

Dad hauled Jo up onto solid earth and Muhammad pointed to where the hill rose and disappeared. 'Go, quickly,' he said.

The toothless man ran forward and shoved Dad's shoulder but three other souk owners grabbed him and dragged him backwards. I didn't look behind me as we rounded the bend, but Jo did.

On the other side, the hill sloped downwards again into a long, quiet alleyway. We found a souk with two high piles of shoes and Dad spoke to the salesman in Amharic, trying to find shoes in the pile that would fit Jo's clown-sized feet. Jo sidled up to me, her arms gripped together across her chest. 'Did you see what they did?'

'Who?'

'The other souk owners. The man that grabbed you was on the ground and they were beating him with sticks. He wasn't moving.'

I twisted my hands together to stop them shaking. My arm felt cold and tight where his hands had twisted around it. Dad, Muhammad and the shoe seller sorted through the pile. None of the shoes seemed to match. Jo had stopped talking.

I saw the dirty green beanie first. He pulled it into his hand as he approached me, drawing his hand through the blood on his head. Muhammad turned aside and told me to ignore him.

'Are you sure? What does he want?'

The toothless man was yelling and waving his bloodied hand at me.

'Muhammad, Muhammad what does he want?'

Muhammad refused to look at the man, pretending to focus on the shoes, but he tilted his head slightly so I could hear him.

'He wants ten birr.'

'Ten birr? That's nothing. That's less than ten cents in New Zealand.' I reached for my bag but Muhammad grabbed my wrist.

'Don't touch your money.'

He turned his face back to the souk but I could see him watching the situation with his peripheral vision. I backed up against the tin wall of the souk, the man still yelling at me.

He seemed to get fed up finally, throwing his hands in the air and backing away, but then re-wiped his hand across the trail of blood snaking down his face and leapt forward, wiping the blood on Muhammad's jacket. Muhammad turned his head in slow motion and stared, appalled, at the bloody handprint. Suddenly, he changed his mind about ignoring the man. Muhammad screamed at him, waving his hands in a shooing motion. Jo shoved her feet into too-small shoes with blue Velcro straps, like the shoes I wore before I could tie laces. Her toes and heels spilled over the edge, but she said, 'It doesn't matter. These are fine. Please can we just go.'

Muhammad refocused his attention. 'This man grabbed your sister. We don't owe him anything. We don't have to leave because of him.'

The man backed off again, huffing through the gaps in his teeth. He looked like he was going to leave, but then bent down, picked up a stone, and waved it in his hand. He advanced again, staring me directly in the eyes.

'Uhh, Muhammad. Muhammad.'

Muhammad turned, saw the stone, and quickly signalled to Dad, who peeled some birr off a roll. The shoe seller shook his hands and said, 'Don't worry, go. Go.'

Dad and Muhammad pushed us down the alleyway, but the man trotted ahead of us, the stone still in his hand. He mimed throwing it, and shouted down the alley. The dense, busy crowd fell silent as everyone turned to listen. Men and women ducked out of their stalls to see what was going on. Thirty or forty men were following us, forming a long column of bodies, and more joined the throng as we passed. The toothless man leapt around the people in the crowd, screaming, and pointing to the blood clotting on his head.

'Dad, what's he saying?'

'Doesn't matter. Just keep going.'

The alleyway opened up to a huge arena where a single dirt road led away from the market. By the time we reached it, we'd attracted a crowd of nearly a hundred people. The four of us backed into a huddle, surrounded. Jo cried quietly. I asked Dad to please tell me what everyone was saying, but he was scanning the road for a bajaj. A huge man, his neck a knot of muscle, broke out of the crowd and whispered to Muhammad. The toothless man still circled us, shouting hysterically to the crowd, pretending to throw the stone.

The huge man was elbowing through the crowd to our left, splitting the group apart as a bajaj slipped through. Dad tapped Muhammad on the shoulder, and said something in Amharic.

Muhammad nodded, then leapt forward and pounced on the toothless man. Dad pushed Jo and me into the bajaj. Muhammad kicked the man's hand, knocking the stone onto the ground. Dad and Muhammad jumped in the bajaj at the same time, and it took off. The crowd dived away to let us through. Dad finally explained that the crowd had been protecting us, that they'd been on our side.

Muhammad said, 'I have never seen that happen before. Never in my life.' He took us to his small hut-style house, his aunt made us coffee, and we bought our gabis from the women in his village.

We had arranged for Muhammad to come by our hotel in the afternoon to take us to Debre Birhan Selassie church, but once we were safely inside the hotel I didn't want to leave. Jo rang her boyfriend and I sat alone in the rooftop restaurant, watching the rust-coloured sunset, and thought how stupid I'd been. I felt disconnected from every nation I'd lived in. I'd always stand out in a crowd here. I'd always represent the Italians, and the British, and the missionaries. I didn't want to be a tourist here. I didn't want to be a scared white girl hiding in another hotel. I'd kept Ethiopia as a reserve home, somewhere I could return to as a kind of birthplace; not of my physical self, but of some early conception of my identity, of my earliest memories. But I have no claim on this country. I have no country.

Muhammad asked if we still wanted to visit the church. I didn't, but I nodded anyway. He said I'd need a headscarf and I happily wrapped one over myself. We walked silently through the streets.

In the trees surrounding the church were brown masses of beehives. When the Sudanese Dervishes burned Gondar, this church had been saved. The smoke reached the church before the Dervishes did and irritated the bees. When the gate was broken down, the bees swarmed out and the Sudanese ran, dropping their torches, swatting their hands about their faces. The churches in Gondar that survived were the ones with bees.

The front door was the men's entrance, and the side door was for women. Muhammad explained that I should leave my shoes at the entrance of the women's door and meet him inside, but when I shook the women's door it was locked. I called to Muhammad but he couldn't hear me. I tiptoed to the corner near the men's entrance and stuck my head around, trying to be as small as possible. Muhammad shook his hand at me, 'Get back, get back!'

'Sorry. I'm sorry, it's just the door. It's locked.'

Muhammad kept waving, panic on his face, and I backed away, my cheeks red. A tiny old man hobbled forward, shaking his head at me and unlocked the door. I apologised as I passed through.

I'd come here for the fresco. Sixteen rows of angel heads painted between the beams of the ceiling. The angels have no necks, only a pair of wings tucked under their chins. They look like bees, like a beehive. My own neck seized from walking with my head bent back.

A memory came back to me. We'd been playing outside in Shishinda, Dijana and I. Mum was nearby. Jo was sitting on a blanket. Suddenly Mum ran towards us, scooped up Jo, and pushed us forward, telling us to run to the house. A small dark cloud was chasing us. The cloud got louder as it gained on us. Soon it was droning around my head. Mum pushed me through the screen door onto the patio and slammed it behind us. She ran her hands over our heads, checking to see if anything was caught in our hair. The dark cloud of bees crowded the screen surrounding the patio. They bounced against the mesh.

The memory returned so suddenly, and so vividly, that I don't know if the buzzing was in my head or from the hives outside.

At the airport the next morning, Jo bought a mug with the fresco on it, and we left Gondar behind.

Axum

There was a strange distillation of light in Axum. A kind of orange glow, like when you think it might be getting dark soon. From the airplane window I'd watched the sides of the Rift Valley stretch apart and dissipate. The green gave way to sand, the colour becoming thinner and thinner. Valleys opened into desert plains.

Our hotel in the desert had five stories, a vast marble lobby, and apart from the staff it was completely empty. We talked in whispers because every sound echoed through the empty lobby. A waiter stared into the distance, mechanically wiping the same bench. The power was out most of the time, except for a few hours when the lights suddenly flicked on. Jo walked around the lobby trying to find wi-fi. At the back of the building, next to the staircase, was an open courtyard where a single goat was tied to a tree.

Jo came back to our room having not found wi-fi. I was reading by the window in the last of that weird glowing light. Children were playing in the street below me.

'I lost a 300-day Snapstreak,' she said, and flopped

onto the bed dramatically.

I said, 'Five days left.'

'I've been counting too,' she admitted.

'Since Gondar?'

'Since Addis.'

It started to rain and the sound of laughter from below vanished in a moment as the street emptied.

'I miss being able to drive, or going to a café on my own,' I said. 'I want to walk down the street and feel invisible.'

'I want a steak,' she answered. 'And Netflix.'

Axum was the first kingdom of Ethiopia. We'd travelled backwards through them, from the newest to the oldest. Our new guide, Alemayu, a tall man who laughed constantly, led us to a site in the middle of town where ancient stelae stretched into the sky. Several were on a dangerous-looking lean.

The stelae were inscribed with three languages: Ge'ez, Greek, and Sabean from the kingdom of Saba – sometimes called Sheba. I had read about these stelae, how the writing on them indicated a culture that worshipped the sun, how one is unfinished, lying on its side, crumbled in the middle, its abandonment marking a sudden conversion to Christianity. So, it remains as it was 1700 years ago, half finished.

Under the stelae are rows of tombs, emptied by thieves. Alemayu ran ahead of us and hid in the dark tombs and we followed the sound of his laughter to find him again. He did this at every opportunity.

When we came up from the tombs a woman approached me with nuggets of frankincense clutched in her hands, shaking them at me. I tried to explain in a language she didn't speak that I couldn't take it on a plane. I didn't know how to gesture the intricacies of getting through customs, so I had to shake my head and walk away, leaving her with her palms open.

We went back to the hotel before the afternoon rains. The goat was still tied up in the courtyard. Jo and I sat on the cobblestones to pat it and the hotel staff poked their heads out the window to watch us. The wi-fi was working, but only in the lobby, so Jo sat in a window seat on her phone. CNN played on the TV, rotating the same story about Trump's tweets that had followed us through every hotel lobby. Jo sat where she wouldn't have to see the goat shivering in the rain, but as she left to come upstairs she saw him being led away by the kitchen staff.

That night, Dad ordered in Amharic and a waiter took the order to a man behind the counter who read it and picked up a giant sickle-shaped knife. Above him, hanging over the till, was the whole carcass of a young goat, dangling by its ankle, like Achilles over the River Styx. He stretched out a limb and hacked off some meat from around the ribs, dropping it onto a scale and passing it through a hole in the wall to the kitchen. Jo and I ate the vegetarian shiro that night.

The next morning, Alemayu took us to the Queen of Sheba's traditional bath – an enormous pool, as wide as the mountain it sat under, where everyone in the city gets baptised each year on Timkat. He drove us out of town to the Queen of Sheba's traditional palace, across from where a farmer once found a cut sapphire in his teff field. I asked him what he meant when he said 'her traditional palace, her traditional bath'. He said he meant there's no evidence to suggest she was ever here, but nothing to prove she wasn't. Archaeologists started excavating Axum, but whatever they found they would remove to their own countries. So Ethiopia banned foreign archaeologists and began the long process of training their own. Until those students are ready, the sites remain unexplored. Only 9 percent of the ruins have been excavated.

'So maybe, one day soon, we will have our evidence,' he said, smiling at the thought, before ducking around a stone wall to hide from us. We found him, giggling, in what was once a throne room. I imagined the Queen of Sheba listening, according to tradition, to a merchant telling her of a wise king named Solomon who knew all there was to know. I imagined her leaving this room, travelling to Jerusalem, and returning pregnant, while Solomon dreamt the sun had left Israel to shine on Ethiopia.

The Bible calls her the Queen of the South, but for most of Ethiopia, she would have been the Queen in the North. She may have been called Candace, or Bilqis, but the Ethiopians call her Makeda, and claim that every emperor, up to Haile Selassie, is descended from her. Some say she had a disfigured ankle – an injury from a jackal. Some say she had hairy legs and cloven feet, like a goat, like a demon. They say a lot of things.

'Now,' said Alemayu, laughing, 'who wants to see the Ark of the Covenant?'

God had asked Solomon what he wanted, more than anything, and Solomon asked for wisdom. In return, Solomon asked God what he wanted, and God asked for a home. So, Solomon built him a temple. He covered it in gold, and carved angels into the beams, and lions and pomegranates. In the middle of the temple, he placed the Ark of the Covenant, the dwelling place of God. He enclosed the Ark within ten thick curtains, protecting the people from God. The Ark, according to the Old Testament, was built by the Israelites after their exodus from Egypt. Anyone who touched it fell down dead, including Uzzah, who had only reached out to steady it.

According to the Ethiopian story, Makeda returned home and gave birth to Menelik, her son with Solomon. At eighteen, Menelik returned to Jerusalem to meet his father, and left with the Ark hidden in his caravan.

Whichever story you believe, this remains: after being established in Solomon's temple, the Ark disappeared from the record. When Babylon invaded Jerusalem, the Ark was either carried away as spoils, or was already gone.

St Mary of Zion, the home of the Ark, is the most holy site in Ethiopia. Before we entered the compound, Jo and I had to wrap scarves around our heads to cover our hair. The walls of the domed church are painted with biblical and historical scenes for those who can't read, and at the apex of the dome is a chandelier gifted by Queen Elizabeth II, which is only turned on once a year.

In a dark, dusty room next to the church are robes that were worn by Ethiopian rulers, brightly embroidered with gold and precious stones. They're hung in rows in a glass cabinet so that only a few can be seen. Ancient books and Bibles are stacked on top of each other in the cabinets. Three-tiered filigree crowns, necklaces, rings and bracelets have been dumped in piles. The silver has oxidised and the gold grown dull and dusty. Alemayu shook his head at the cabinets. 'If I ran this place I'd display these things properly, and I'd turn the lights on so you could see them, and maybe then the tourists would come back.'

The Ark is in one of two small chapels in the back of the church compound. Both chapels are perfect squares. One is older but bigger, with a golden dome. The second has high glass windows stained with a turquoise geometric pattern. Both buildings sit atop a high stone wall, which is enclosed behind a wrought iron fence. Only one person knows which of the two chapels houses the Ark. 'If you wait, you might see him,' said Alemayu. Someone had climbed the high stone wall and was crouching on the tiny ledge outside the gate, his hands gripped around the iron bars to hold himself up, his face pressed against them. As we watched, an old man with a long grey beard, in a turquoise robe and white shamma, came out of the older chapel. He spoke to the man on the fence, held his hand over the man's head, and then flicked his shamma over his own face, and returned to the chapel. Alemayu turned to us. 'We are very lucky to have seen him.'

The only person who ever sees the Ark is the virgin monk who spends his entire life, from the time he's chosen, within this iron fence, keeping constant vigil and burning incense over the Ark, so that the presence of God residing in the Ark is never alone. When one monk dies, another is standing by to replace him. Jo asked if the guardian was allowed to watch TV in there, and Alemayu rocked back against the fence, his hand over his jiggling pot belly. I asked if any have quit. Alemayu looked confused at this. 'Why would they quit? It is the highest honour.'

'It must be lonely.'

'He is in a room with God.'

I know how kings write stories of their own divinity, so they are not only obeyed but worshipped. Theologically, the Ark has served its purpose. With Christ, a new covenant was made, and we are now the dwelling place of God, and not the Ark. I am God's house; I am the temple now.

But I had to wonder: at some point, in all the

hundreds of years, hundreds of virgins alone, didn't one of these men reach out a hand, touch the Ark, and live? If he lived, then it is an empty box, void of God. Yet, not one of them has thrown off his robe, jumped the fence, and walked out of St Mary of Zion.

I looked up at the doves circling the chapels. I hadn't seen doves anywhere else on our trip. I asked Alemayu if they're trained to do that, to circle the dome. He said, 'What doves?' and looked up. He'd never noticed them. He didn't answer my question, but instead told us a story. He was once hired by a man who'd travelled from America to see the Ark. Alemayu led him through the compound, telling him the same stories he'd told us that day, but the man didn't want to see the crowns, the old books, the piles of ancient jewellery. He'd come to test the Ark; to sit outside it and see if he felt anything. They sat together on a bench by the iron fence. The American had closed his eyes, let out a breath and said, 'OK, I'm convinced.' I asked Alemayu if he'd felt anything that day. He said no.

When I came to Ethiopia, I doubted their claim to the Ark. Even as I'd entered the gates of St Mary of Zion, I still doubted it. But suddenly I found myself wondering, if the Ark isn't here then where is it? And if it's here then who brought it? And if Menelik brought it here, then who were his parents?

I asked Alemayu if he believed the stories about the Queen of Sheba and the Ark. He looked up at the doves circling the dome. 'I was unsure for a while,' he said.

'But at some point, I just had to decide, so I decided to believe.'

I wonder if Menelik had a home, if he felt split between nations. Did he wonder if he was from two places or no place?

People stared into our bajaj as we headed back to the hotel, and I knew they were lumping me together with the many tourists who've passed through this place, cameras in hand, hoping for a glance of the virgin monk. Another white face in a passing window. I wanted to stop and explain that I'm not that kind of tourist, that I was from here in a way I wasn't from anywhere else. This was my home.

But maybe I'm not different. Maybe I'm just like every other tourist. The only difference is that I was stupid enough to think this would feel like coming home.

Lalibela

In the tenth century, the Ethiopian kingdom was one of the richest in the world, dominating the trade routes with hard crystals of frankincense. In the Amhara region, a child was born and a cloud of bees covered his face. The bees told the baby's mother her son would be king. He was named Lalibela, which has been translated as both 'honey-eater' and 'the bees recognise his sovereignty'.

Lalibela took the throne by force. Shortly afterwards, an angel came to him in a dream and showed him a new

Jerusalem, high in the mountains; a new River Jordan; a new temple. I imagine him waking, honey on his fingers.

Lalibela named the new capital after himself and began work on a labyrinth of churches. The churches were dug not out of stone but into it, carving out the white space. Each church is a single piece of stone. They sit deep in the earth. I stood on the ledge above and looked down.

Our guide, Tesfaye, said archaeologists have calculated how long it should have taken to dig out the churches, and how long it actually took. There's a disparity between the two. They were built much too fast. Tesfaye explained that the reason it took half the time it should have is because men worked the days, and angels worked the nights.

In Lalibela, we're 9,000 feet above sea level. It's hard to breathe this close to heaven.

Pilgrims climbed these mountains on their knees and I crawled here through a tunnel of memory that gets narrower at the end and falls away behind me. I thought I had been here before. I had a memory of standing on a ledge like the one I was on, looking over a rock face, seeing a cross-shaped church cut into the ground. But it isn't possible that I remember this. We never came this far north.

Memory is a false door, a house with a trick ceiling. It's glitter in the wind. It's the only record of our life and it's wrong.

Tesfaye pointed to a moss-covered pool and said, 'This is where infertile women are dipped for healing.' Jo asked where infertile men get dipped and Tesfaye laughed and continued on.

In a cleft in the wall were the preserved bones of two pilgrims. Their skin hadn't fallen away but had blackened and hardened over the bones, wrinkling like leather. I asked Tesfaye how they're so well preserved, exposed like this, to air and tourists. He didn't know. He said, 'They shouldn't be. They should have turned to dust.'

He led us along a high ridge between churches. There were no rails, nothing to stop us falling. During Timkat, the priests form a line across this ridge. They dress in white robes. They sing in Ge'ez and wave their arms in unison.

I asked, 'Is this safe? Has anyone ever fallen?' Tesfaye laughed, a smile like the Rift Valley. 'Of course no one has fallen. The angels would catch them.'

On my way back down, I spotted a hole in the ridge, bees flying in and out.

Tesfaye touched his forehead then his lips to the door post of the church before we went in. He picked up a torso-sized drum and pulled the strap over his head. Goat skin was stretched over each end. One end was wide, the other narrow. The body of the drum was covered in fabric printed with flowers and big red love hearts. Leather cord was wrapped around the body of the drum. Tesfaye tapped the wide end, bending his knees and dipping down as he sang.

He said, 'The wide end of the drum represents the Old Testament. Hear how deep the sound is? How dark? The smaller end is the New Testament.'

He tapped this end and the sound rang out further. It was lighter, the bright sound of a new covenant.

Running his hand over the base he said, 'The fabric is the body of Christ. These strips of cord, they're the whip marks, the spear in his side. By his stripes we are healed.'

On the way back from the churches, Dad bought a silver Lalibela cross, and laughed as he walked away from the salesman, who had turned to speak to his friend. Dad translated what he'd heard them say: 'That white guy thinks he can speak Amharic.'

That night, in our hotel room, I was reading a *New Yorker* article about power cuts in Sub-Saharan Africa when the lights flickered and went dark. With no wi-fi and no moonlight, Jo and I got into our beds at 7.30 and talked about how strange and complicated this trip had been. She reminded me of the time we tried to join a GP after moving to New Zealand. I'd handed over my birth certificate and been given membership. Jo explained that her birth certificate is Ethiopian, and she has an Australian licence and passport, but she is from New Zealand. The receptionist looked puzzled. She frowned at the Amharic writing. 'I can't read this,' she said, handing it back. 'I need some proof that you're from here.'

71

'My parents were born here. My whole family is from here. I'm a New Zealander.' Jo threw her hands up. 'What can I give you to prove it?'

The nurse threw her own hands up. 'Sorry, I don't know.'

When we first moved back to New Zealand as adults, leaving our parents in Australia, Jo had put a little box on her dresser and in it were her toothbrush and toothpaste, floss, a travel-size bottle of Listerine, and one of those round mirrors on a stick that dentists use.

One day, Dijana and I decided to hide the box. We don't often mess with Jo because she's stronger than the two of us combined, and on more than one occasion has dragged Dijana through the house by her ankle, throwing her outside and locking the door. But the box bothered us. Jo refused to explain why she didn't just keep her toothbrush in the bathroom like a normal person.

After hiding the box under bed, we sat giggling in the living room, waiting for her to notice, but we stopped laughing the moment Jo saw the box was gone. She was hysterical. She screamed at us to get it, to tell her where it was, that it wasn't funny. I dove under the bed and pulled the box out. Dijana put it back on the dresser in exactly the spot where it had been.

'Look, it's back where it was,' Dijana said. 'Exactly the same spot. See? We're sorry. We won't do it again.'

Jo stood over the box rearranging things, hiccupping. We backed slowly out of the room. I made three teas, which we drank in silence until Jo said, 'Look, we've had a very unsettled life. I'm twenty and I've moved nineteen times across four countries. But I've always had a toothbrush. That's what you take with you when you go somewhere. That doesn't change, and I just wanted to keep everything together and make it nice, like how people make their homes nice.'

I hadn't realised how our life had affected the other two. I remembered the time we were part of a community, and a time after, when that community was gone. I thought because they were too young to remember a time before and after, that they wouldn't have been affected in the same way. But, while I've spent my life looking for some sense of belonging, Jo has spent hers looking for something that will remain the same.

I told Jo the story of how in my early twenties I'd started having a recurring nightmare. On a trip home, I'd been cutting tomatoes and telling Mum about the dream. 'We're in Bishoftu, and I'm in the car waiting for everyone. A monkey drops from a tree onto the bonnet of the car and we stare at each other. Then another monkey drops down. I hear a thud as another one lands on the roof. Suddenly, the car is covered in monkeys. They're shaking the car, pulling at the window wipers. It's terrifying. I have the dream every night.'

As soon as I looked at Mum and saw how she'd stilled over her cooking, I knew what had happened. 'We only left you for a moment,' she said.

The memory came flooding back in. I could see the monkeys jumping on the car. 'You went back for something.' I remembered screaming and hitting the window to make them go away, yelling for my parents to come back.

'It was less than a minute that we were gone. Your little hands were bashing against the glass. I've never heard anybody scream like that.'

My sessions with Lesley had reminded me of this, and at our last session I'd finally wanted to talk about Ethiopia. I'd said, 'I have this feeling sometimes, when I try to remember. It's like there's this white space in my mind, like the fog that used to bury the house. Sometimes it feels like maybe that white space isn't empty but full. Too full to open. Like in cartoons when they throw open a cupboard door and everything that's been crammed in comes tumbling onto their heads. Is there a way to make myself remember?'

'Sometimes we forget things for a reason,' she said. 'It's not always a good idea to go rummaging in that cupboard.'

'What if I just want to know? For interest's sake. I know there are gaps in my memory. I want to know what's true?'

'How do we know if any memory is true?'

I was starting to wonder why I was paying so much for these sessions.

'Alie,' she had leaned forward, 'have you ever considered writing about this? Maybe even going back?'

In the morning, fog pressed in at the windows. I opened the doors to the little veranda, swished my hands through it, feeling like I was under the ocean. I remembered, in Shishinda, trying to catch the mist in a jar, and I wished for one now. Trying to describe Lalibela is like trying to take a photo of the moon: never as bright or beautiful.

Now I know my memories of this country are wrong, I have lost them and I can't get them back. I'm caught in a wind that won't let me land. No soft earth will have me. I hover over the waters.

Back in Addis, we waited for Dad to exchange some money. Elias had picked us up again, but he'd wandered from the taxi to stretch his legs. I was exhausted, peopled-out, tired of being looked at and discussed. A man stuck his head through the open window of the taxi and said, 'Hello American.' Jo sighed. I answered the man, 'Heougeyenligaj.'

'French?' he asked, 'Parlez-vous français?'

I answered again in gibberish, smiling so he'd think I was trying to communicate.

'German?' he said.

'Yehagneulam.'

The man gave up and walked down the street to the woman selling chewing gum and khat.

Jo laughed. 'Couldn't you have thought of that two weeks ago?'

We asked Elias to take us to one last place. He drove us into the walled compound where we'd lived before being sent to Shishinda. Here, finally, was something I remembered. Dad knocked on the door of our old house but no one was home. He reached up on his toes and looked through the window.

Someone had left a pair of rollerblades on the lawn and I wondered who they belonged to and what their life was like.

Elias drove us to his friend's shop so we could buy presents for people back home. The shelves and tables were stacked high with lengths of fabric, paintings on goatskin, clay pots, woven baskets, meskel crosses in brass and nickel. Jo held up a goatskin painting of Jesus sitting behind a plate of injera, six disciples on either side, his palms outstretched. 'Alie, look,' she called. 'It's the Last Injera!' She laughed and added it to her pile on the counter.

As we built up our collection of gifts, a crowd was forming outside. A man held a laminated map of the world that didn't show New Zealand and yelled a price through the windows. Others had their faces to the glass. I bought my things quickly. Elias gestured for Jo and me to hold out our wrists and he clipped a bracelet onto each of our arms. 'My gift to you, so you always remember your friend in Ethiopia.' Then he drove his taxi close to the shop door and pushed people out of the way. We ducked our heads and ran through the crowd, falling into the car.

Elias slammed the door behind us as the crowd pressed around the car. He turned around from the front seat. 'You should change your names to Kardashian.' Then he put on his favourite Teddy Afro song, one I was starting to like too, and drove us to the airport.

Wellington

I caught up with friends in Wellington who wanted to hear about the trip. On the way to the bar no one looked at me, or pointed me out. No crowd of children followed, wanting to shake my hand. I was invisible again. I couldn't get my head around how 'back' I was. I couldn't collide the experiences together, or understand how I was just there but now I was here.

By the end of the night, my friends still hadn't asked about the trip and I was glad, because how could I explain?

At two in the morning the most sober of our group organised Ubers and, while everyone waited on the street, I drifted away. A man approached me. He wore a green bomber jacket and dark jeans. He was tall and slender. I recognised the aquiline bone structure.

'Your necklace,' he said. 'Is it Ethiopian?'

I touched the brass meskel around my neck and nodded. 'I got it in Addis last week. Which part are you from?'

'Gondar, but I grew up in Canada and moved to New Zealand a month ago. I only lived in Ethiopia for three years.'

'Oh, well I'll tell you about it some time.'

He laughed and leaned on the Perspex wall of a bus stop. 'Why were you there?'

I said my parents were aid workers, and distracted him from further questions by asking if he'd found the Ethiopian restaurant in town.

My friend called me over and the man said, 'Let's get injera some time.' I entered my number in his phone and he said, 'Ameseginalehu.' As I walked away, he said, 'When I saw your necklace, I felt like I was home.' I didn't know what I'd do if he called. I hadn't even meant to give him my real number, but he never rang.

There had been a grass fire in Shishinda. No one in my family can remember how it started, or how it was put out. I'd forgotten all about it until I noticed the charred grass in one of the home movies and suddenly remembered the way it had crunched under my feet, collapsing to nothing, as fast as candy floss disappearing in your mouth. I shifted my memories, remembering that when we'd run from the swarm of bees, and when Miserite and I would carry buckets of water to the builders, the grass hadn't been green but black. Now I remembered how we'd slid over the grass and felt it turn to powder, and stain our feet.

Today, I went for a walk beside the golf course and froze at a smell that hit me like a time machine, making me feel like I was five years old in Shishinda again. There are so many Shishinda smoke smells: fireplace smoke,

smoke from frying corn on a brazier, smoke from coffee roasting on a plate. This smoke smell was acrid. It had an edge to it. Something peppery.

I looked around expecting to see smoke coming from someone's chimney. Instead, I spotted a fallen log at the edge of the golf course. Surrounding the log was burned grass. I had a sense memory of that particular type of smoke, though the event that created the memory is lost.

I'm glad we never went back to Shishinda. At least this way there's one sacred place in my memory, however flawed those memories might be. It's one thing to revisit an old home and find it gone. It's another to find it never existed. The memories I thought I had of Addis are gone, but I get to keep Shishinda, and I get to go back to it when I see a flash of bright green mountains with no end, or a bright bird, or smell smoke or injera, as if some weird magic from my childhood is sending me a smoke signal, or Morse code from flashing mirrors, on a very distant hill.

Shitfight

The grenades aren't shaped like pineapples, as I'd thought they would be, but more like cans of Coke. My hands shake as I pick one out of the tin box. It could be a cake tin, or a box of chocolates. The bombs are in ordered rows.

The pins are more complicated than in the movies. You could never pull them out with your teeth. (This information is met with collective disappointment, akin to when we learned that shooting from the hip was not an approved firing position.) You pull the pin as far as it will go and then twist your wrist slightly further than is comfortable. Resist the compulsion to brace the grenade against your stomach to help you twist.

A grenade is three pieces. Pin, bomb and lever. It's not the pin that activates the bomb. The pin releases the lever. The separation of the lever activates the bomb. There's a corporal next to me whose job it is to drag me around the trench wall and jump on me if I happen to drop the grenade and throw the pin. I stare at my hands, grenade in one, pin in the other, and remember a time in school when I unwrapped my sandwich, threw the bread in the bin and raised the paper to my mouth.

I throw the grenade, and watch the lever fly away. The corporal and I duck below the trench. Sound pounds over us, now a solid thing. I could reach up and run my hands through this sound. When the sound dies back, there's a soft pattering of falling earth and shrapnel. The corporal lifts his head over the trench, swearing and holding his hand on his heart.

'Try throwing a little further this time.'

In the recruitment interview they asked if we could ever kill someone. The correct answer is, 'If they were a threat to Commonwealth people or property, then yes. Of course I could.' A boy in the year above me at school had trained for months to get into the army. When he was asked this question, he said no and was told he didn't need to wait around for the physical. For me, it was easy to say the words, words being all they were. I was only signing up for the gap-year programme. I wouldn't be in the army long enough to be in that position. This was a temporary solution until I worked out what I really wanted to do. I wouldn't fall for the propaganda. I knew how these things worked: I'd read Wilfred Owen.

The bugle plays at 6am. We rip both sheets off our beds and stand in the hallway with the sheets over our shoulders. We yell our numbers in turn. One of the first things to get used to is hearing my own voice so loudly. The yelling bursts the capillaries in our noses and they bleed, off and on, for the first week. After the bugle and the ripping and the yelling we are given fifteen minutes to dress and make our beds, ruler in hand, measuring the part of the sheet that folds over the duvet, the placement of the pillow from the head of the bed, and the extra rug that is folded on the end.

As we get further through training the fifteen minutes are reduced to eleven and then nine. The movement and the measuring and the obeying lead to a suspension of thought that leaves no room for anxiety or indecision. Thought is replaced by a narrow consciousness that zooms in on the pulling of laces through boots and the synchronised lifting of mattresses. We're being trained not to think. The point of these three months is to break us down and build us up again as soldiers. They don't want someone on the battlefield who will pause or question orders. They want soldiers who will obey. This suspension of thought is useful when I realise the showers don't have doors.

The platoon that lives above us is instructed to take all the furniture from their rooms, carry it down the stairs, and reassemble the rooms on the parade ground. They're given ten minutes but they take eleven. They're told to carry the furniture back to their rooms and start again. Each time they fail, the time limit is reduced. They repeat the exercise until a recruit drops his end of the bed on the stairs, curls his arms around his knees and rocks against the stairwell, saying, 'There's not enough time, there's not enough time.' His suitcase is returned to him and the other recruits help him pack it. A different recruit goes missing in the night and is found marching down the highway in his pyjamas.

I get infringed twice in one week: the first time for not starching my slouch hat well enough, the second for leaving a piece of paper on my desk. When rust is found on my bayonet the infringement is upgraded to a charge. I want to explain that it wasn't my bayonet, that all the bayonets in the armoury were redistributed at random before the inspection. But I'm standing on a white line being yelled at, forbidden to make eye contact. There's no designated time for explanation, and no point if there were. So, I get up at 5am and march around the parade ground wearing a pack carefully measured to be one-third of my weight. Corporal Steele, the only person I've ever truly hated, follows behind.

'You're a retard, aren't you, Recruit Benge?'

'Yes, Corporal.'

'What are you, Recruit?'

'A retard, Corporal.'

There's comfort in knowing he also had to get up at five. Bombardier asks me why I'm such a shitfight (noun: Someone who is bad at everything they do; everything they touch turns to shit). The name sticks. It attaches itself to me and I hear it when I fall through the netting on the obstacle course, when I realise I haven't seen my rifle since the last time we stopped for a break, when I panic about running through an underground drain half full of water. 'Shitfight' is staccato. It's sung like a nursery rhyme, and whispered under a breath as I pass.

My own name falls away and Shitfight takes its place.

People ask me why I'm here, in this space where I so obviously don't fit. I tell them I thought I knew what I'd wanted after school: an internship, a desk that I could put framed photos on, a career in advertising, but it wasn't what I'd expected. I want basic training to be over, but not like I'd wanted those months to be over. My future had stretched out before me: the same day, the same bus ride, the same nine hours. I struggled for breath in the never-endingness of it all. Here, at least I don't wake up sad, count down the hours from 8am, and cry behind my sunglasses on the ride home. Perhaps that's what keeps me here while people who aren't shitfights have breakdowns in stairwells. Perhaps they had a second option, something to return to. But I can shut out the insults and dull their edges in a way that I could never dull monotony. I may be a shitfight, but at least I'm not bored.

I can't remember what I'd imagined the army would be like. Whatever I dreamed about beforehand was quickly excised by the bright, dusty, out-of-breath reality. It was my friend Sophie who first dreamed up the plan. We would enlist in the gap-year programme together, get cool Myspace photos, save our money, and go travelling when it was all over. It was these prizes that kept me going as I performed the nightly jog around the block that was my training. I was dreaming, with no thought of war or politics, and I needed the hope of something different. Then Sophie didn't get in and I had to go by myself.

Bombardier gives us this: 'You're on a mission in Iraq. You and three others. It's crucial that you aren't seen. On the last day of your mission, a young girl wanders into your camp. She starts to cry and run for home. What do you do?' We say, 'Bug out.' We say, 'Abandon the mission.' When he shakes his head, we say, 'Restrain her somehow until we're done and then let her go.' These are not allowed. Bombardier waits, but no one will say it. We're given a talk about hesitation.

I'm surprised by how much talking there is. I learn to yawn with my mouth closed and rest one eye at a time. We're given talks about honour and tradition. About sacred duties and administering justice. During the latter I avert my eyes from pictures of children in an Iraqi town, their skin blistered and bubbled, like melting plastic. The results of chemical weapons. They tell us about landmines, how they're designed not to kill but to maim. That particular lesson is about the Ottawa Treaty, which outlawed the use of landmines. On a PowerPoint slide is a list of non-signatories: the nations that ignored the treaty and continued to plant mines like seeds to bloom under children and farmers: China, Russia, Iran, North Korea, Pakistan, Saudi Arabia.

Other lessons are on the Anzacs, the Rats of Tobruk, the Victoria Cross. The talks could be divided into 'Who is your enemy?' and 'Who are you?' The will to win is rewarded. A lack of aggression is shamed. We watch videos of tanks driving in formation, soldiers running and diving behind walls, all in slow motion with Jimmy Eat World's 'Hear You Me' playing in the background.

At school I'd craved an opportunity for radicalisation. In primary, my friend and I would change our names to sound like hippies. One week I would only answer to Sunshine Daydream; the next, Mountain Flower. We would play suffragists without any understanding of the concepts of voting or violence, having not yet identified oppression.

The radicalisation was an objective desire. It had no subject or direction. It was an end in itself, rather than a means to an end. Something about the stories I'm told during training gets in my blood. They touch the part of me that wants to belong to a community and be part of a movement. Besides, there is shame in not believing their ideology, and I've had enough of being shamed. Soon I'm running my hands over my scalp as my head is shaved, long hair floating to the ground. I'm standing on parade on Anzac Day. A swell of pride and a forgetfulness. *Dulce et decorum est, pro patria mori.* Lest we remember.

The lines on the targets are arranged in a disruptive pattern. Enough black against yellow to suggest a human form, but not so many lines that it's obviously a person. The hope is that in another context, another time, we'll see only this suggestion of a person through our cross-hairs.

There's a recruit named Cameron who, for some

reason, we call Dick. His interest in death is awkward. His questions about it reveal something in himself that we're uncomfortable being near. He asks Bombardier if he's ever killed anybody. Bombardier sneers at him and says, 'There's something not right with you, Dick.' But as he walks away, he says, 'I don't know. You drop a bomb from a plane. It explodes. What do you think?' I wonder what Bombardier sees on those strange nights when you wake in a half-dream state and things come back to you, larger than they are in the daylight. Does he see a door open in a plane and a flash of light and fire?

During basic training I can't imagine ever being out of here. How was it that once I could get in my car and drive somewhere? How did I govern my own time? The day we graduate there's a feeling in the air, like on the last day of school when we'd stack the chairs in towers and talk about holidays. As I get on the bus to leave, Corporal Steele yells over the crowd that he's going to call my next posting so they know to expect a shitfight.

The bus takes me to a holding platoon in Melbourne where I'll sort out everything I need for corps-specific training. The first job I'm given is to write my will. After that, I'm led to my new bedroom and I'm alone for the first time in three months. When my door shuts for the first time, I feel like I can't take a deep breath. I fold socks under the door so it won't close fully. I go to the shops to buy my dad a birthday present but I can't remember how to decide.

I finish my training in Melbourne and I'm sent to Townsville where the air is so hot it feels like hands around my throat. There are only two seasons here: the hot season and the wet season. They're both hot, it's just that one is also wet. A stranger tells me he once saw a bird die in midair and fall from the sky. I live in a building with artillery boys and I sleep with a metal bar under my bed. An email goes around telling us to watch out for the crocodile that lives in the river by the gym.

Townsville is a garrison town and the civilians here call us Army Jerks because we drink too much and start fights at the Strand on hot weekend nights. They don't smile at us. It's suggested we avoid public transport and travel in twos. Our shaved heads and strong arms give us away. I'm blasé about the warnings, overconfident, until something is slipped into my drink and I spend a night staring at taxis and telling people I have stars in my wrists. This is the fifth time I've changed cities this year and sometimes I look for landmarks to remind me where I am.

The eighth of March hovers in my mind as the day I enlisted and the day I can leave. Yet as March approaches I find I'm not ready to go. If I stay, I could get a post in Brisbane, a deployment in June. A deployment means I could buy a house, or go to uni without a student loan. I have to decide.

There are hippies dancing and waving signs outside the base in Townsville. One shakes a sign at drivers that says, 'Honk if you want peace.' Another, 'Refuse to serve in Afghanistan.' I drive past on the way to Subway and think how almost a year ago I might have done something like that. The next month, civilian protesters sneak into Talisman Sabre, a joint exercise between Australia and America. They try to take videos of our training but they're caught at the fenceline. People are getting angrier and security is tightened on base. We talk in groups about how civilians have no idea what's going on over there: how we're training the Afghan National Army, equipping them to look after themselves, and then we'll leave. We say war is the means by which peace is achieved. We bolster one another's opinions and they flourish. The eighth of March arrives and slides past. I'm posted out to Brisbane. I prepare for a war I don't understand and I wait as, one after another, deployments are promised and then fall through.

In Brisbane I learn that if anyone was to invade Australia it should be at 7pm when everyone on base is drunk. During one of these 7pms I meet Steve. He likes me because I'm the only girl here. I like him because he has those muscles with the veins running along them, because he has a higher security clearance and tells me secrets, and because he'll be gone soon. He's off to Afghanistan as soon as his promotion comes through. He says cooks are safe over there. He'll get put on sentry and patrols, but it's a non-combat role. I tell Steve a cook at training told me that if insurgents get all the way to the kitchens, they've broken through every line of defence. The cook had said, 'Wait till they flood in, wait as long as you can, then blow up the gas tanks. Get right up close and you won't feel a thing.'

Before Steve leaves, a cook from our battalion is killed. He was on sentry duty with a recruit of the Afghan National Army. Security clearances are no match for gossip networks. People pass the story back and forth. The recruit must have killed him because the shot was in his back, and because the recruit disappeared into the desert on the back of a waiting motorbike. I thought of those conversations in Townsville, how we'd believed one another about war bringing peace.

Men die in the Afghan spring, when insurgents come out from their winter hiding places. In the Book of Samuel it says, 'In spring, at the time when kings go off to war.' It's unnerving, how unchanging war is. We call it the 'killing season'. We lack the poetry of the prophets. Every killing season, smiling photos of dead soldiers appear in the papers. We get released from work to attend more talks to bolster us again. We're shown more pictures of the Taliban's victims; more stories circulate: 'Look what the bad man did. Look how they treat their women.' We're fed a hero fantasy.

But it's a man in green who walks me home one night and tells a lie to our friends. He says I waited by the door, taking my time with my keys, and then invited him inside. Men in green send the texts that roll in like thunder: 'Steve deserves better than an ugly slut like you.' Steve doesn't believe the lie and I wait for him to defend me. I wait and I wait. He laughs when our friend runs up behind me and pulls my skirt into the air. 'Whore' is written on my door with little stick-figure diagrams drawn all around it. The diagrams, or I suppose they're portraits, could be a disruptive pattern. The suggestion of a person. I stare at the Sharpie marks against the blue paint and wonder, who is my enemy? In which country does he live?

I drive to my parents' house and start looking up universities. I end up reading about the Ottawa Treaty and find the United States on the list of non-signatories. I am out of love with this. I should already be gone.

I read in my field notebook, 'The F1 grenade has a kill radius of six metres. Casualty radius of fifteen metres. Contains 4000 ball bearings to maximise damage upon detonation.' I can't remember which lesson this is from: 'Who is your enemy?' or 'Who are you?'

I don't remember leaving. I remember starting university, and relearning how to buy groceries and be alone, but walking out of base that last time, handing in my resignation, doing final medicals, these memories are gone, in the same way that I wake in the morning with no memory of falling asleep.

Three years later I find a box in my grandparents' cupboard. It's full of letters from my Nanna's uncle, who died in the war. The last letter says, 'Don't worry about me. Something seems to tell me that I will come through all right and all will be well.' He died on the ninth of September 1918, aged twenty-one. *Dulce est*, blah blah blah. War is like a card game that the old teach to the young.

I heard that when Steve came back from Afghanistan he'd have panic attacks whenever his name was called. He was diagnosed with an allergy to coffee.

Immigrant

I've heard stories about Croatia all my life. The country shimmers in the background of yarns about my great-grandfather, Didie. There is no family story that isn't, in some way, about Didie. In the stories, the rushing flame of his anger is set against his quiet afternoon kindness: the young immigrant stands in contrast to the old settler. Every time we get together, someone will say, 'Remember the time Didie had a tantrum at the orchard, throwing himself down, wailing, beating his fists against the ground like a child.' Another will say, 'Remember the time his car broke down at Mt Roskill and he chased after the other cars, shaking his fists and shouting, "You bloody bastards. You won't help an old man!"' My mother remembers sitting at the kitchen table, swinging her legs, while he made her jam on arrowroot biscuits and Ribena in milk. He used to carry an envelope with a smiley face on the front that was filled with Valium. The stories of him are woven so neatly, into such a bright image, that on the week of Grandma's funeral I thought I saw him at the mall.

I nearly called out before remembering he's been dead almost my entire life.

He insisted everyone call him Didie, even though the Croatian word for grandfather is dida, and the people who call him Didie are his children and in-laws. I was a teenager before I realised his real name was Ljubo. Didie is pronounced the same as 'did he', but as it would be said in a laconic, Kiwi way that skips over the H. The conversation often goes:
'Did he?'
'Yeah, Didie.'
'No, *did he.*'
'Oh, yeah he did.'

It's impossible to know how many details of the stories are true, because embellishment is a Croatian art form. Didie's is a nation of unreliable narrators. This has flowed through the blood to me: the compulsion to make every story bigger. I add details that sound better, funnier, and then I forget I added them. They take a shape and colour of their own and I transpose them into memory.

Didie was born in Podgora: a thin belt of green at the bottom of sheer, unproductive, grey slate mountains. Didie was told at fifteen that his family couldn't afford to feed him. So, he went into town, borrowed money for a ticket, walked 70 kilometres to the harbour in Split, and got on the next ship for New Zealand. He never saw his parents again. His family was exiled to Egypt during World War II. Didie's father got off the boat, took one look at Alexandria, and fell down dead. At that point, Croatians had already been catching ships to New Zealand for thirty years, as Yugoslavia had slid almost seamlessly from Balkan War to World War, when people travelled for survival rather than for experience. They were after a gold rush, but they didn't go to Hokitika or Otago. They went to Northland for the dirty yellow shine of kauri gum. They arrived in waves, landing in the morning and digging their first holes in the afternoon. Hard work was their national export. Eventually, they'd take photos of themselves with their hair slicked back, wearing gold watch chains, and send home for wives.

As a child, I was constantly being uprooted and replanted somewhere else. We went from Auckland to Tauranga, Tauranga to Ethiopia, back to Tauranga via several months in Kenya, and to Australia, where I lived until moving to Wellington as an adult. There was always too much distance between myself and any culture I had a connection to – the space was too wide to cross. I didn't grow up kola dancing on Sundays, dressed in red and white, I don't know the songs, or play the tambura. I only have the stories.

Culture persists around death. It's where rituals are trotted out and find their significance. So, it wasn't until my grandmother's funeral that these stories I'd heard, the secondhand culture, filled up with bones and blood. It put on clothes and came to find me. I'd never considered the fact that this group of people I'd been hearing about for most of my life were alive somewhere. I thought they were across the sea, perched over the Adriatic, not here on a grim, grey Auckland morning at the Glen Eden Catholic Parish. Here, trilling with their hands clasped and their mouths stretched into Os. Here, with names like Steepa, Tea, Nedika, Petar. Here, where the man flashing lascivious looks at me from under heavy, lowered eyebrows is my cousin. Here, where people are my height! And I don't slouch to make myself smaller, less visible.

My paternal family's history is somewhat higher on the class scale, though considerably lower in physical stature. While my father's ancestors were selling their title of nobility, my mother's side were pissing on each other's olive groves. Jill, my aunt from my father's side, comes to the funeral for moral support but her measured, polite, blue-blooded voice is a foot and a half below everyone else and can't be heard over the volley of talk above her. I make a misstep in a joke about our height, saying we should carry poles like at the rollercoaster. 'Must be this tall to ride.' I realise too late what I've said. A gleam flashes in my cousin's eye.

My father is one of the pallbearers and he grips the end of the coffin. He stands on the end, solemn, facing a different way to all the others. At the cemetery, we're one pallbearer short. We find a replacement and Grandma is lifted out of the hearse but then we realise Grandpa is missing. Grandma goes back in the car. We stand around, bracing against the cold, trying not to fight. Grandma waits patiently. She no longer needs to hurry, or to be pushed along. Grandpa shows up (he'd gone home, not wanting to use a public toilet), but my cousin and uncle, both pallbearers, have driven away to look for him. When the key characters are finally in the right place and we have at least five pallbearers, Grandma is trundled out again. Grandpa is astounded by Jill's umbrella, its colour! Its girth! She tries to direct his attention back to Grandma, who is being lowered into the ground, but his eyes are up, his mouth open. He is reasonably deaf and yells over the sombre crowd to Jill, 'Where'd you buy it?' Jill whispers, 'The Warehouse', and points to the casket. Meanwhile, the sixth pallbearer wanders alone through the wrong cemetery wondering where everybody is. My aunt leans in to me and says, 'This is nothing. At Uncle Clem's funeral, he was too tall for his own grave. He had to be put to one side while shovels were found. We were put to work making it bigger.' We joke that our family puts the fun in funeral.

The Croatian gumdiggers had a habit of only telling other Croatians when they found a productive spot. The New Zealanders weren't mining the gum as fast as the immigrants were, so in 1910 it was decided that only British subjects could hold gumdigging licenses. The

Croatian gold rush was over and the diggers flooded Auckland's countryside, forming suburbs of orchards, sticking with those from their own provinces. Those from Podgora settled in Oratia. They had dinners once a week at the Marinovich's and dances every Sunday, prospecting for someone to marry. They rebuilt their community in the Dalmatian and Yugoslavian Clubs, dancing in their peasant costumes, hopping and spinning, stamping in their black boots, arms akimbo or linked around each other in circles. They helped each other pick the fruit on their orchards so no one would have to pay wages to anyone else. Once, someone brought their friend to visit the orchard. The friend was stunned by the dark-haired girls picking peaches and asked someone to teach him 'Nice tits' in Croatian. He was taught 'Ja sam govno' – actual translation: 'I am shit'. After practicing a few times, perfecting the pronunciation, he took off, bellowing his new phrase, his arms spread wide, wind blowing his hair back, yelling to the left and to the right, to the beautiful peach-picking women, 'I am shit. I am shit.'

At the funeral, my sister asks if it's a coincidence that Oratia is almost an anagram of Croatia. Heads turn to the sign, mouths open. After all this time, no one had even noticed.

Someone at the funeral asks if my uncle Joe was named after Joseph Marinovich, Didie's father-in-law. We nod our heads; we know this one. Joe was named after

Joseph, my sister Jo was named after Uncle Joe. Nothing to see here. Joe doesn't nod. He quietly explains that he's named after the first Joe in Didie's heart: Joseph Stalin. My sister blanches. My Kiwi grandfather, in his too-loud voice, tells a story of the time, on a lunch break, when he sat on apple crates with the family and listened to them laud communism, celebrate it, miss it. Grandpa stood up from his crate and announced that they were 'Full of shit'. Circling each other in the orchard, Grandpa said, 'Fight me if you want, I was captain of the Auckland rugby club.' Grandma later found she'd been struck from the will.

My family are wound tight. They're anxious, vengeful, manic depressive, obsessive compulsive. The family that remains in Croatia have been at war with their neighbours for over forty years because my grandma's cousin tripped on the neighbour's bike and threw it into the Adriatic. From them I inherited the ability to twist small details into wider fears that loom, black and stormy: a cloudscape blowing over a bright day. They lay siege to each other, holding each insult close. They've borne grudges to the grave, and stolen inheritances. They've disapproved of and neglected each other. Yet, they helped each other on the orchards, and met for lunch every Sunday. They exercised shocking generosity, and when babies were born they got speeding tickets on the way to the hospital.

In 1991, back in Croatia, Serbian neighbours started packing their things and leaving in the night. When the war finally broke, my cousin, Đulijano tried to enlist but, because of his education, the army office told him, 'We'll need you to fix things when this is over'. Podgora filled with refugees from Dubrovnik and Didie sent every piece of clothing he could find. Đulijano's father risked his life sailing a tiny boat past Serbian war ships to get aid to Dubrovnik. Didie died halfway through the war, before Yugoslavia was dismantled into bickering nations. When it was over, letters were sent to New Zealand saying, 'You only call yourself Croatian now. There is no more Yugoslavia. You make sure you're proud to be Croatian.' Đulijano was sent to visit us and to make sure we were saying the right thing. Members of the Dalmatian and Yugoslavian Club split off and formed the Croatian Club. Every member of each club was already Croatian, but the divide was over a name. A line was drawn between the new guard and those who refused to change. Where you kola danced on Sundays became a political and ethnic statement, a matter of nationalistic pride.

Those who emigrated rejected aspects of their culture to fit into their new homes. Some anglicised their names, adding Hs to the spelling, and taking the dashes out of Đ. Didie made sure his children spoke English and, when each generation asked him to teach them Croatian, he said, 'No. We're New Zealanders now. You speak like the New Zealanders.'

It's the following generations who take hold of culture. We experience it academically, collecting stories, researching our family's origins, and meeting cousins over the internet. We grasp at the things our ancestors had to flee from, longing for the grey slate mountains and the thin, anaemic food that had meant their exile. We learn to make the boozy donuts, and blitva – which is simply silverbeet boiled until it's limp and off-looking. It tastes like water left too long in tin. My mother hates blitva but insists on making it. She's dedicated sections of her garden to growing silverbeet and complains bitterly every time she eats it. We turn to the shreds of culture that are left to us and say, 'Tell us who we are.'

From here

Walking through Akatarawa Cemetery, Nanna says, 'It's important you stay in touch with your roots. You've been away so long. You need to reconnect, now that you're back.'

'David Benge' is carved into the stone above '1820–1907'. If this were a scene in a movie I'd peel back the moss, sit here awhile, maybe say something. But I don't want to touch moss, and I have nothing to say. Everyone has walked on and legacy is a shifting ground. I walk by six generations of bones and wonder what they'd think of me.

.

They weren't the first white settlers. Someone must have been there drawing the sketch. Three Benges, all in a row: David, John, Nicholas. They're wading onto Petone foreshore, carrying their wives across the water. It's a bad man who lets his wife's skirt get wet. Back then you could sail all the way down the Hutt River. When the house in Petone burned down, they sailed down the river and started again, clearing trees from Te Marua to Akatarawa. It was 1840. The ink on the Treaty was still wet enough to be smudged.

.

I still remember the stickers I was playing with when my sister told me we were moving to Australia. Blonde mermaids with sparkling emerald green tails, which I stared at until tears blurred their image away.

.

What colour is your childhood? What temperature? Mine is blinding white sky, salt breeze, sand searing feet, ten mangoes for ten dollars, a snake in the kitchen. But further back, before the packed boxes and the shimmering heat, there is a wet green, a yellow spread of gorse, brown sugar on tamarillos, flipping ferns to see the silver laid against their undersides. A rhythm beats its way back through the tunnel of memory: 'tin of cocoa, tin of cocoa, tin of cocoa car door.'

.

People ask where I'm from and I want to say, how far back do you mean? Do you want to know where I live now, or where I was born? What if both are different from the places I grew up? What if I told you my baby teeth are scattered across four nations, and sometimes I think about them and wonder where they are? I imagine one incisor rolling down a mountain in Ethiopia, the other lost somewhere in the Tauranga library, or a cuspid blowing across an Australian desert, a molar leaned against an acacia tree in the Mara. Instead, I say, 'I'm not sure. Nowhere I guess.'

.

The plane tilts, and I get a parting shot of bleached sand; the same pristine beach I'd glimpsed fifteen years ago when I first arrived here. I look away, and Australia slips off my shoulders like a coat I've worn out. In Wellington, the wings catch the wind and toss the plane down the tarmac. I have left the country I'd lived in the longest, but I have this long-forgotten feeling of coming home. I stop the car in Upper Hutt and we take jumping photos by Benge Crescent, Benge Hall Reserve and Benge Park.

I haven't seen my grandparents' home in over a decade. It still smells the same. The furniture hasn't moved. The same spoon is sitting in the sugar bowl, the inexplicable plastic container of coins is still in the pantry. I want to cry over every tiny thing I recognise. I've only ever left places; I've never returned to them.

I move into a house that shakes in the wind and has rain dripping down the walls.

.

The pharmacist looks at my script. 'Benge, eh? That's an old Upper Hutt name.' I wonder if David Benge would have a collective noun for daughters: a shame of daughters, a ruin. I imagine him smoking his pipe in hallways as, one after the other, his daughters are born, that old Upper Hutt name growing thin as bones, blowing away.

.

My grandparents cut us up like cadavers, apportioning each body part to different branches of the family. Those with Benge features are the purebloods. I have the Poulson dark hair, the Salisbury nose. I'm tall for a Benge. The branches are marked by a series of maiden names, those streams that fed the river. The pieces get smaller. Feet, eye shape and knobbly knuckles find a home. My sister is told she has Hazelwood fingernails.

.

As much as I'd tried to hold onto those concave vowels, they eventually popped outward. They took on hard edges and people stopped asking me to say 'fish and chips'. Now, people laugh when I say 'Māori'.

'Maowwri?' They imitate. They repeat it properly, that flick of the tongue to the back of the palate, the tripping 'r' sounds, the 'o' where you thought there was an 'a'. I attend a te reo class at the local marae but the other students are already fluent. They use words I used to know that now feel strange and convoluted in my mouth, like trying to speak around a mouthful of stones.

.

In Upper Hutt, I meet a girl at a party and realise we're related. I see ropes twisting around us, tying us together. We trace the lines back. She says, 'So only third cousins. Nothing really.' She is accustomed to a wider net of self and this is not remarkable to her. But there, on her hands, it's unmistakable: the Hazelwood fingernails.

.

The Benges have for an heirloom a kingdom of only each other, a set of no members. I'm being prepared by the over-seventies to carry the torch, to hold to imperialism; to believe that because of those Benges carrying their wives over the water I belong to this place. I try to push the stories away. I steer conversations away from subjects of heritage, Akatarawa, the old Benge homestead that's now a café. I think of that photo in the library's heritage collection: David Benge standing by a wagon full of logs, not smiling, his hands behind him. He's looking at me. He knows I left.

.

The strands of my family's history wind backwards, on and on, to that bracket in time when white sails brought white men, and the Benges gave names to already named places. Now that I'm back, I'll belong to no place. I mouth the anthem because I can't remember the words. But I'm building a house in Te Marua. I'm planting peach trees and maybe I'll be here when the peaches grow. I'm learning to brace the house against the southerly winds. Maybe one day I'll be here long enough to know the weather patterns, I'll know the names of the roads, and where to find secret carparks in the city. Maybe then, I can walk by all those bones in the cemetery and say, 'I'm from here.'

Have You Ever Seen the Rain?

Dad isn't the type to chat to strangers, except when I'm drowning. In those days, there were three thermal pools at the foot of Mount Maunganui. We would walk up the mountain and I would imagine I was Heidi, then we'd swim in the hot pools. The big pool had a step in the middle so it suddenly plunged from shallow to deep. That day, I'd pulled off my arm floaties because the hard plastic edge pinched my skin. I'd bounced along the shallow end, towards Dad, and the stranger he was talking to. I never saw the man's face, only skin, a stomach. I didn't realise they were standing beyond the step until the pool floor vanished from under me. The water pushed up over my head in a rush of bubbles and muffled sound. There was only blue and bubbles and the wobbling shapes of legs. I pushed up from the bottom of the pool, kicking back into the noise and the light. I had one second to breathe and thrash my arms, to make whatever sound would come out. The water rushed up again. Bubbles streamed out, leaving me. I would die.

Dad's hand shot through the water, planted me back on the step, and he returned to his conversation. I stomped to the other end of the pool, back to where I'd left my floaties, and sulked in the tepid water, warm as a body.

.

The drought began the year we moved from Tauranga to the Gold Coast, the year the century flipped over. That summer was so hot the candles in our house melted and drooped over. It had been a thousand years since there was such a failure to rain. The Queensland government declared a day for us to pray, which seemed an unusual thing for a government to ask, but it was cheaper than pumping water from the Brisbane River. We prayed on Friday and it rained on Saturday, but not enough. The second problem was that the dam was too small.

At my new primary school, we shared theories about what was at the bottom of Hinze Dam, now the level had dropped so low that the rotting branches of old trees were visible above the water. Chris said there was a whole town under there, and when they built the dam some of the townspeople refused to leave. They stood in their doorways as the valley filled with water.

Chris said: 'Soon we'll be able to see the church steeple, the chimneys. We'll be able to walk through the village and the last of the water will wash out the bodies of those who stayed.'

'How long have they been there?' I asked.

'Oh, hundreds of years. Thousands.'

In the second year of the drought, we could only water our garden on Wednesday and Saturday. People dobbed in their neighbours for having suspiciously green lawns. We were encouraged to get shower timers so we knew when we'd exceeded the recommended two minutes.

In the third year, my class went camping at Lake Moogerah. We were quiet as the bus circled the lake. It had become a muddy puddle. The earth along the banks had cracked, like in those World Vision ads. I had been quietly enjoying the drought, the drama of it. It made me feel special when I told my New Zealand friends about it, the friends I was slowly losing touch with. For the first time, it occurred to me that the water really could run out.

My sister visited her pen pal in Tauranga and almost cried over their dripping tap. She put a bowl under it to show the family how much water was wasted. They said, 'I guess we never thought about it.' Their eyes flicked to the windows, rain pouring down.

When she came back, we went to Hinze Dam for a picnic and she told us how the family had left the tap on while brushing their teeth, and before drinking tea they'd poured hot water into their cups to pre-warm them, and then tossed all that water down the sink. We covered our faces in horror. No one remembered to bring cutlery to the dam so we scooped salad into our mouths with our fingers. Between the water and the treeline was a steep bank of mud, like a soap ring in a bath, where the water had receded and receded. I remembered what Chris had said about the church steeples, the chimneys.

The nurseries closed because they couldn't water their plants. A suicide hotline was set up for farmers. Flames swept over the dry hills. On a long car ride, I felt sick. Mum told me it helps to look at something green, but there was nothing.

After ten years they called it the Millennium Drought, either because it was the worst drought in a millennium, or because it dragged us through the first decade of the millennium. Both were true. In the newspaper I read about an eight-year-old girl who had never seen rain. I thought of Tauranga, a place I'd never returned to, which had taken on a sacred quality in my memory: a lush, cool paradise. I remembered walking to the dairy under a purple sky, and how warm the school pool had been when it rained, when I'd sit low in the water and watch the drops plinking on the surface.

When Mum visited her parents in Auckland, her photos were of green fields. She told us, 'I made them stop the car. You wouldn't believe how green it was. Radioactive green. Felt-tip green.'

When the drought broke, the rain evaporated on the hot road and hovered above the asphalt in wisps of mist. At first, we said, 'Hallelujah!' We ran into the rain; we took photos of it. The trees in the dam were reburied. The rivers refilled. We said, 'We're saved!' But then we said, 'Wait. Stop. This is too much.' Water spilled over the dam wall; the rivers broke their banks. Every field flooded. The water washed cars off bridges, then it washed away the bridges. A local boy was sucked into a storm drain and had to relearn how to talk.

Toowoomba – nearly 700 metres above the sea, and miles inland – was hit with a wall of water that exploded homes. Seven and a half billion tonnes of water flooded down the Great Dividing Range and smashed into the landlocked city. A man filmed the creek that ran through town as it rose over its banks, under the parked cars, lifting them up one by one. They flooded down from upstream, stacking together like bumper cars as they drifted. The man filmed someone running to his car to rescue it and yelled, 'Don't, don't, don't. Mate, just let it go!' People were rescued from their roofs. An entire house ended up in the middle of a field and no one knew where it came from. The insurance companies told the people of Toowoomba that what had happened was technically an inland tsunami, and they were only covered for floods. Months later, my parents picked up a hitchhiker who'd lost his business in the flood and was off to look for work in Brisbane. He was down to his last $1.70. My parents scooped out all the coins from the ashtray to give to the man. They checked under the mats in the car and between the seats.

I moved back to New Zealand when the drought ended, as half of Australia drowned and the other half burned. The summer I arrived, New Zealand declared a drought. The Wainuiomata hills turned brown and I wondered, 'Am I the problem? Do I bring this with me?'

The drought was short-lived and I learned the joys of daydreaming in the shower. The water here is free. I learned why people say that rain 'lashes'. It is like a whip pulled back, thrown forward, snapping against the windows. People watered their lawns and washed their cars in the driveway. People here grew flowers.

I moved into a house by the water and it looked different every day: sometimes like glass, sometimes like poured concrete. One night, during a storm, the ocean was level with the road and I couldn't tell where it began. A wave crashed right over my car and I was sure I was about to die. The next morning, a house on the waterfront had a caved-in garage door, a huge stone resting innocently in front.

That first spring, orcas swam in the harbour, seals wobbled up the banks. I walked on the pebbly shore picking up bits of sea glass, feeling like a woman in a romance novel. The street exploded with blossoms, as though someone had burst a bag of icing sugar. The village smelled like flowers, the kinds that could never grow in Queensland. A neighbour's peach tree grows over her fence. I reach up and pick a peach off the tree on my walk to work. I can only do this because it rains.

I was in a Thai restaurant when the pendant lights started swinging. There was a roaring sound in the distance and a rattling. Strangely, my first thought was that a giant was shaking the building. I secretly like earthquakes, in the same way I liked the drought in the beginning, but that night I thought about the tsunami evacuation signs I'd seen around Wellington. I imagined waves crashing through the windows, and became obsessed with clips of the Indonesian tsunami. I watched an interview with a woman who had gone diving that morning and returned, having missed the whole thing, to find her hotel gone, her family gone, the note she left explaining where she was; all washed away. I dreamt I was in the backseat of a car and turned to see a wall of water. It rose up through the floor, bubbling under the doors, climbing over my feet, my knees.

My next house was on a mountain. The harbour looked so much bigger from that height. A sperm whale showed up in time for Matariki and the fireworks were cancelled so we wouldn't scare her. Half an hour after the Kaikōura earthquake the street outside my house was lined with cars full of people fleeing the tsunami zone. The local pastor drove to his church in the middle of the night, loaded up with packets of bacon. Families filed into the church and the pastor made hot chocolates and bacon butties until it was safe for them to return to their homes in the valley below. I got a week's leave from work because the shop was flooded. The morning after the earthquake I sat at my kitchen table and stared at the harbour. How do we survive at all when we require such a fine balance? It kills us when there's too much, when it's too fast, when there's not enough. It makes the flowers grow and the street smell like spring. It sends us whales and seals and sea glass. It pulls back and rushes forward. We can't even hold it in our hands.

Flame Trees

2008

The first time we met, you asked if I was a lesbian because my head was shaved. You said, 'Don't you know guys like long hair?'

I found out you had mean nicknames for all of us. I told Jake that I despised you and complained that we had to spend two weeks on exercise with someone who was so bogan that he says 'fair dinkum' unironically and has not one but two tattoos of Australia.

That exercise was the culmination of our corps training before we were to head to our postings. Somehow you had your posting already. You were going to Darwin straight after the exercise was over and you couldn't wait. You hated the cold.

Before we went out bush, we had to spend a few days at the Albury base for testing, which no one minded because the cook there was the best in the army, and the pub was subsidised. On the bus to Albury, we argued across the four seats separating us. You said I was ugly and I said you were probably inbred. Sarge put *Full Metal Jacket* on the TV at the front of the bus and you, Bradley and Gallagher cheered at the bit when the guy shot himself. You told a story about the time your wife was making you dinner on Valentine's Day. She asked you to go buy some milk and you spent all night in the pub. You said she'd taken your dog when she left, and you didn't miss her because she was a bitch but you really loved that dog. Later, I was carrying my bags to my room and you sprayed shaving cream on my hair.

You were talking to someone across the other side of the pub and Gallagher said, 'I think he likes you.' I said, 'He can like all he wants. So long as he does it from over there.'

When you joined our group later you told us you grew up on a cattle station in Argadargada. You taught me how to say it properly. You said you hadn't seen rain till you were eighteen. You said you once met a group of Aboriginal people who didn't know white people had come to Australia. One of them taught you to play the didgeridoo. I noticed how tanned your arms were.

Bradley wanted to show everyone how fast he could drink Cruisers. He ran around the pub challenging people to a race to the bottom. Soon he was stumbling towards me, pointing in the direction of the barracks. He said something like 'Home' and 'How do I get?'

I caught him around the waist and tried to lead him

back to his room. His eyes were closed, his head slumped on top of mine. He was so heavy and I couldn't get him up the stairs. Suddenly his weight lifted off me, and there you were, slinging his arm over your shoulders. You told me the elevator didn't go all the way to the top with Bradley, and that he once said the moon must be closer than Darwin because he couldn't see Darwin from where he was sitting. You put him in bed while I got a bowl from the kitchen and put it on the ground where he could reach it.

When everyone was leaving the pub later you said we should check on him. We found him sleeping in his vomit, the clean bowl under his arm. He stank of urine. You said he'd be embarrassed if he knew I'd seen him, so I went back to my room and you helped him get in the shower.

Later, you knocked on my door. You said you'd wanted to steal a beer glass from the pub so you'd snuck it into my bag. Sure enough, there it was. I gave it back to you and you turned it in your hands and asked if I liked Bob Dylan because you'd been watching this documentary about him and you could start it again from the beginning if I wanted to watch too.

I said, 'I love Bob Dylan.'

Do you remember all this?

During the exercise you and I were put in different teams. We got up early and worked all day and we didn't stop working until we went to sleep. We hardly got to talk except for that thing with the sullage. Remember the

118

sullage? I drew the short straw so it was my job. It was a makeshift drain made of grass and sticks. I had to pour the dirty dishwater over the grass so the water would go through but the scungy bits would be caught on top. After a few times, I'd get rid of the grass and lay some more down. One day you helped me carry the water to the sullage. I should have taken off the grass already, but I hadn't because it was disgusting, so the water didn't drain fast enough. We had to stand there and poke the grass so the water would go through. Later you found me and said you'd made me something. You led me to the sullage and it was brand new. You'd laid the grass out so neatly and you'd found some branches I could use to scrape the grass off without touching it. When I poured the water over, it went straight through. Later I noticed you'd moved your sleeping bag next to mine.

On the bus ride home, you sat next to me even though there were so many free seats. You tried to convince me your music wasn't terrible by making me listen to your favourite songs. You played 'Flame Trees' and I said, 'Do you think Jimmy Barnes has two tattoos of Australia? Do you think he says "fair dinkum" unironically?'

You said, 'You've read him wrong. This song is about remembering someone your whole life.'

You played Springsteen and said, 'He's fun every now and then, in a nostalgic way, but I get over it quickly.' You played Lee Kernaghan and said, 'Let's sing real loud and piss everyone off.'

When we got back, we went straight to the mess and then everyone left for the pub. You held me back and said, 'Let's not unpack. Let's drive around for a while. Let's sleep on the beach.' You said you'd bring your didgeridoo but you forgot it, which I thought was weird because it was the only thing you went back for.

The night before you left, we sat on the back of your ute and talked about how we wished we had more time. You said you'd try to get better at using email and I wrote my Hotmail on your hand. I was wearing your jumper and it smelled like cigarettes and cologne. Before I gave it back, I sprayed my perfume on it so that later you'd smell it and feel sad.

I told Bradley I hadn't heard from you yet but it was probably because you were driving through the Outback and wouldn't have reception. He told me you were going to get your dog back before heading for Darwin.

I said, 'Isn't it a bit late for that? His wife left years ago.'

He laughed and said, 'She left a few weeks ago. She leaves all the time.'

When I was a kid, I'd jumped down a sand dune and landed flat on my back. There had been a whooshing sound as the air shot out of my lungs. I remembered that as Bradley spoke. I recalled the feeling of a chest closing in on itself. I tried to call you but you didn't pick up. You could have given me a chance to explain. I didn't know.

This isn't what I do. Did you think I knew? Did you think about me when you saw her again?

Gallagher said he'd been with you when you saw Argadargada on the map on the wall at the dentist. You thought the name was funny. You practiced it so you'd remember.

Gallagher said, 'You really think a wise old Aboriginal woman taught him to play the didgeridoo? Come on.'

I remembered how you'd forgotten to bring it to the beach.

He said, 'There's no way there are Aboriginal people who don't know about white people. Wouldn't they have seen roads? Wouldn't they have talked to each other? Think about it.'

He said 'He had a thing going with Bradley. A bet.'

'What kind of bet?'

'What kind do you think? You were asking for trouble going around like that, like you're as pure as the driven snow. You were an in-between thing for him, while the wife's away. You got two weeks. Be happy with that. Anyway—' he ran his hand over his jet-black hair and handed me a cue '—want to lose at pool?'

Bradley got posted to Darwin as well and he left a few days after you. Jake, Gallagher and I got sent to Townsville.

It had been months since you left. For a while I still thought you must not have reception. I wondered if

121

you got a new phone and lost my number, but then you messaged Jake. You said you hated Darwin. Jake read me the messages. At the end he read, 'Say hi to Alie for me. Tell her I miss her.' This was when phones could be unlocked by pressing the home button and the asterix key. You probably still have one like that. Jake left his phone on the couch in an ad break and I wanted to know if you'd really said that. I wanted to see your name on a screen.

You hadn't mentioned me. Jake was a good friend. I let go of you then.

2009

You rang me at the end of the year. You said, 'I've been sick. I've been in hospital. My wife came to visit me and she brought my dog.' I asked what was wrong and you said, 'Oh, you know. This and that.'

I asked why I hadn't heard from you and you said, 'Yeah, sorry. I made a mistake.'

I didn't ask about the bet because it would be so easy for you to lie about it and I'd only believe you if you said it was true.

You said, 'Let's leave. Let's just go away.'

I said, 'But I'm buying a house, I'm hoping to get a deployment soon. Besides, I'm with Gallagher now.'

Should I have told you about Gallagher? Should I have told you that I was to him what you are to me: someone standing apart, just out of sight? He's settled for a portion of me, as I would have taken a portion of you. He told me things you said about me and I don't know what to believe. He'd once asked me, his hands gripped around my wrists, what I'd do if you came back. If I'd told you this, would you have taken his weight off me, slinging his arms over your shoulders?

I said none of this. You started getting quieter and I said, 'I'm glad you called.' You thought I was saying goodbye but I wasn't, I only wanted you to know. But still, I was relieved when you hung up.

We were told a group from Darwin was being sent to Townsville to help us on an exercise. I saw Bradley in the crowd and asked if you'd come down too. He was surprised I hadn't heard. He said you'd been in hospital on suicide watch. After you were released, you went back to work for a few days, then you walked into the bush and never came back. No one knew where you were. I went back to my room and pressed my hands into my eyes and took deep breaths because Gallagher was coming down the hall and he'd been so upset when I told him you rang. He'd said, 'Thank you for your honesty,' as though I was confessing something, and his hands had trembled. He'd pushed me and I'd hit my head. He'd pinned me to the wall, his weight crushing me, so I'd know that he was stronger than me, that I could breathe because he let me.

You should have told me. I should have left when you asked.

2013

You finally got Facebook. I'd looked for you occasionally, but you have such a common name. Then one day, there you were. I tried not to add you. I thought I should wait for you to add me, but I've never been one for self-control. When you messaged me you wrote, 'I went AWOL in 2009. Couldn't stay there anymore. I live in Alice Springs now. It's beautiful here. It's a good life.'

I said, 'I've thought about you a few times over the years. I've wondered how you were.' I tried to write quickly so you wouldn't see I was typing for too long. I sent a message that was too long. I was embarrassed by it. I said, 'Whoops, that turned into an essay.' Two months later you replied: 'Sorry I didn't get back to you. Hope you had a good Christmas.' You leave me grief-blown.

2018

I mentioned you to my friends the other day. I said, 'I knew this guy, a long time ago.' On my way back to the car I tried to think how long it's been since I thought of you. Now Gallagher is gone, Jake and Bradley are gone, and so are you.

A week later you messaged me. I felt like I caused this by saying your name. I felt like a witch. You said you remarried and had a son, but this wife left you too, taking your son to Wagga Wagga. You had to move there to be close to him. I asked how you could stand to be so close to where we did boot camp, and what it's like seeing little buzzcut recruits marching in their groups of three.

You said, 'Maybe I should move to New Zealand. I know a girl there from a thousand years ago.'

'I wouldn't want to tear you away from Wagga.'

'Just ask me, darlin'.'

I left you on read so you'd know what it's like.

I decided that the next day I would ask you for answers. I'd say, 'Why are you back? We got two weeks a decade ago, yet here you are, still.' I wanted us to remember the stories from that trip, like when Bradley thought the moon was closer than Darwin. I'd say, 'What am I to you? Am I a Springsteen song you feel like listening to again? Am I a bird smuggled into your coat? Each time you go, you leave me flat on my back with missing you.'

But then it occurred to me that I might have made you up. I saw you spinning in the air, your arms out like Sailor Moon, while I transformed you into someone else, stitching you together. It occurred to me that I don't know you.

I stalked through your photos. There was your wife. She's pretty. She has long blonde hair. You have her initial tattooed on your ring finger. And there you were, playing the didgeridoo.

I didn't ask you my questions. It was my turn to leave. My last reply was dismissive; no questions for you to respond to. I wrapped things up. You read it at 9:20. You didn't say anything. I wish you'd try harder.

I went to a house-warming the next night and drank too much Scrumpy. I found myself slumped on the couch, chin on my chest, checking my phone.

Twenty-seven organs

Franz Gall noticed that people with a certain eye-shape were good at memorisation. The eyes bulged more than usual, as though they couldn't believe what they were seeing, as though they had the capacity to draw everything in and lock it away. From there, Gall mapped the landscape of the brain, the rivers and mountains, the spines of alps. He said the brain was a mass of twenty-seven organs, and the dips and peaks of the skull mirrored the enlarged or undeveloped sections of the brain.

.

The top of the brain holds the capacity for hope, and belief in God, which seem so much like each other. Care for offspring is centred in the back of the head with wonder on either side, like Wonder Bread. The back of the brain is a children sandwich. Sense of time rests above the eyes: the part of my head that spikes and throbs when I feel time running out and I have too much to do. Cautiousness is a small wedge in the temples, that part that feels softer than the rest, already concave, as if waiting for its moment to break.

.

I can picture Gall sitting in his office, surrounded by the skulls of humans, dogs, and birds. I can imagine him getting stuck on an idea, putting a hand to his own skull in frustration, and finding in it the answer he was looking for. Not a falling apple, but a head falling into a pair of hands.

.

The higher classes used phrenology to justify their superiority and formed a language from the planes of their scalp. They called themselves 'high-brow' for the smooth, sloping forehead that indicated a capacity for science and literature. They were 'well-rounded'. They had developed the right brain organs. The lower classes were happy to find that the organs could be exercised. They could improve themselves and rise through the ranks; it was possible to pull themselves above their stations. Phrenology provided aspiration. It was used to justify slavery because someone decided the skull of a black person indicated that the over-developed organs were caution and veneration, showing a tendency to need a master.

I wonder about the people who paid for this service. Phrenology could provide an answer to a question, but not a solution, like taking a Buzzfeed quiz: we feed in information about ourselves and are amazed when the same information comes back in a simpler form, like it's cracked our code. The complexity of our existence is reduced to one of four options, and we walk lighter because we know which type of pickle we are. The self is known. We look to categories to tell us who we are. We always have, since zodiacs, since humours. Are you black bile or yellow bile? Blood or phlegm?

I picture a nineteenth-century woman slipping into a tent at the fair, and I wonder what she wants to know about herself. What makes her leave her house with the money in her pocket? Maybe she wants to know what kind of person she should marry, or whether she'll be able to love her children, or what she might be capable of if she were allowed a different life. Maybe she just wants someone to pull the pins out of her hair, hold the weight of her head, and run fingers softly over her scalp.

I've looked at the sections of the brain and I can't see where love sits. Should there be a part of my skull that beats like a heart, or flutters like a breeze at the curtains? Sand and soil, the matter of the earth, isn't counted on a map, so perhaps love is the matter of the brain, the pink squishiness that might burst if squeezed. Or maybe love is the fluid that holds the brain in suspension and cushions it against knocks. That care, that's a kind of love. When I was twelve I broke my head. Blood and brain fluid spilled over the rocks I'd landed on. When I tried to get up, it slid down my neck. Perhaps I lost too much, too much of that love, and my body couldn't produce more.

.

If I rested my head in your hands, if you moved my hair out of the way, and fit calipers around my skull, would you be able to tell me why I didn't love you? You were so easy to let go of. I could finally take a deep breath.

.

We've developed a language from locating things in the body. The ancient Hebrews believed love was felt in the guts: 'I love you with all my bowels.' People spoke about the heart before they knew its function, so I've wondered if they weren't referring to an organ but to the centre of a person. More like the heart of an artichoke than the heart of the body. People said I should stick with you because you had such a big heart. By which they meant more the symmetrical cartoon heart that I used to draw in my maths book, with wings on each side and a halo. Not the gory, wet, kicking thing. You once placed my hand over your heart so I could feel it racing, and it was so corny I wanted to leave you right then, though you were only trying to say that you loved me. I imagine you swollen with heart, holding it over my face and suffocating me with it. I got so tired of carrying it around like it was a sparrow that had crashed into my window. I think I wanted to hurt you.

.

There was that time we went to the dive bar in Frankston, and you were doing nothing wrong, nothing annoying. You hadn't repeated a joke, or tried to impress me with how fast you could down your beer, but I looked at you and felt nothing. If you had stayed or left my body wouldn't change, neither heart nor bowel.

.

Maybe I loved you like a brother and missed you like an amputated limb. Every now and then I go to lean on it and find it gone.

.

Unlike the heart, we can't look at a brain and see how it works. We don't see thoughts running along a production line before being pumped around the body. But maybe I can slip into a tent and have someone measure my head and tell me about my life. Perhaps they'll make a chart so I can see, with little static images inside the skull: me engaged in different activities with varying levels of ability. The phrenologist might pull at his beard, and poke a stick at the chart, showing me which sections to exercise, and maybe the surface of my skull will shift and change, that fluid flooding back in. But for now, we walk away from each other and I can barely make you out.

Three winters

Jo knew someone who knew someone whose roommate was throwing away his old TV. She rang me and said, 'It'll take ten minutes. It's so close. When else can you get a free TV?'

I said, 'But it's dark and I literally just put *Pride and Prejudice* on.'

'Colin Firth or Matthew Macfadyen?'

'Colin.'

'If you come, I'll watch Colin with you on my new TV. Please? I can't carry it by myself. And what if they're murderers?'

The guy who opened the door said his name was Gary and did we want anything to drink. The house was dark and cramped. The little light there was struck Gary's exposed midriff. Someone had left their laundry in the machine too long and the clothes smelled like piss. Three flatmates nodded their heads at us as we passed. We each took a side of the TV, pretending we were fine to lift it so Gary wouldn't offer to help. We dragged it to the curb and took selfies with the TV while we waited for a taxi.

The taxi driver didn't help us get the TV out of the boot because he was annoyed that our trip was so short and he'd only made $10. A British accent called out 'Jo', and a head of fluffy, yellow hair flounced along behind the garden wall. Jo's neck started to go splotchy. She tucked her chin down before he reached us and said, 'That's Harry.' And then there he was, trying to edge me over so he could take my side of the TV. His hands were soft, and I felt weird touching them. He tried to carry the whole TV by himself but wobbled underneath it and I rushed forward to catch the side he'd pushed me out of. Jo trailed behind with the cord, red splotches blooming up to her chin.

We got the TV to her living room and Jo said, 'Wow, thank you, Harry. We could never have got it up here without you.'

Harry said, 'Anytime, anytime. Whenever you need me.' And then he paused for a bit and repeated, 'Anytime.'

Eventually I waved the *Pride and Prejudice* DVD and said, 'Well, it was nice to meet you, Harry,' but he didn't leave and started quoting the movie.

'No lace. No lace, Mrs Bennet. I beg you.' Jo laughed and slapped her knee, which I'd never seen her do before.

She said, 'Miss Eliza Bennet, let me persuade you to follow my example and take a turn about the room. It is so refreshing.' They laughed and stared at each other until Jo looked away. The splotches were circling her face and had started to broaden across her cheeks. She said, 'Alie, Harry is from Oxford.' I told Harry I'd always thought it would be fun to sit on a bus in Oxford and listen to people's conversations, and Harry told us about a student who wore a black nightgown everywhere like he was at Hogwarts. We agreed that being smart can make people a bit weird. Jo invited him to watch Colin with us but the TV didn't work.

I said I'd catch the lift down with him. Jo leaned on the door and Harry looked at her and smiled as he clicked the lift button. When the doors slid closed, I asked him if he'd lived here long. He said, 'Mmhm', and got out his phone.

Jo told me they'd started dating. She said he was so smart and he was studying mathematics and he gave her his jacket sometimes. When they walked together he stood taller, trying to match Jo's height.

A few months later I got on the bus at Carillon Ave. He climbed on at King Street. If I spoke to him I'd have to make conversation for ten to fifteen minutes, depending on traffic, so I ducked my head and pretended to be texting. He pulled the student newspaper out of his bag and held it at face level, but didn't turn the page once. When the bus was nearly at his and Jo's building, I realised we'd be getting out at the same stop. I thought about staying on until the next stop and doubling back through Chinatown, but I'd be late for my appointment. I jostled forward early so he'd be behind me at the doors, and then it would be on him if he didn't say hi. We stood next to each other, him slightly behind me. As we got out he stepped on the back of my jandal and I fell off the bus step. I said, 'Oh, Harry. I didn't see you there.'

He said, 'Yeah, weird.'

'You guys should come over for dinner sometime.'

'Yeah, maybe. Sometime.'

'Well, see you,' I said, and we walked in the same direction for one long minute. When he had gone, I texted Jo and said, 'Not once has he asked me how I am.' She must have told him because a few days later I walked past him at uni and he said, 'Alie, how arrre you?' Later he told Jo that he'd been making more of an effort with me.

Harry went home at the end of summer and Jo got drunk and slept in her wardrobe. When I visited she'd taken all the shelves out of her fridge and was scrubbing furiously, her milk going warm on the bench.

She said, 'You know, I'm fine. I'm just trying to keep busy.' Then she stopped scrubbing and her shoulders started shaking and she said, 'Don't look at me.' She cried with her head and shoulders bent inside the fridge. I didn't know what to do, so I pushed the fridge door closed, as far as it would go, and she held it, as shut as possible from inside.

She said he'd asked her to move to Oxford. I didn't say anything.

She said, 'You don't know him, and you've never tried to be nice.'

'I have tried. Remember when I made dinner for you

guys and he talked about himself the whole time and he made that joke about Julia Gillard? About the carpet matching the drapes? I didn't say anything even though I wanted to. I was awake all night thinking about what I should have said.'

That winter was freezing. We visited our parents to help them move house. Jo pretended to be weighing up her options, making a list of pros and cons. She tried to make us believe that she was at least torn between him and us, but we all knew she was putting money away.

Harry's mum sent Jo a text saying, 'Don't worry about towelling robes. We've got plenty.'

I said, 'What's a towelling robe?' We decided it was something British, and that it was a relief to not have to worry about it.

We were eating Korean barbecue when Jo said, 'Remember that time I put the wrong address in the GPS and I drove for an hour before realising? The GPS just rerouted me and I found my way back. So maybe I'm going in the wrong direction now, but I'll eventually reroute and it will all be OK.'

'So you want to consciously make a bad decision?'

'I don't want to make a bad decision. It just happens that the decision I'm making is most likely a bad one. But it's one I want to make. And then I'll reroute.'

When we were paying I said, 'That day, the GPS

day, you had a panic attack and went into a pharmacy to ask where you were and you were crying so much you couldn't breathe. Remember that?'

On the way to the airport, Jo started to finally seem worried. 'I have to live with his parents, and he'll be living an hour away at uni, and I won't know anyone.'

I said, 'It'll be fine,' even though I didn't think it would be.

She told me she cried the whole flight and the air hostess kept slipping her packets of cookies. At Heathrow, Harry was there with a sign and some flowers.

His parents fussed over her, making sure she was warm enough, comfortable enough, had enough towelling robes. I Skyped Jo and she was wearing my dress that I thought I'd lost.

In England, winter hit quickly. Three weeks in and the snow was stacked against the house. She said that when Harry's parents heard her coming down the stairs they leaped off the sofa and pretended to be making breakfast so they could eat with her. She said, 'They try so hard, but I know they've been waiting all morning. They don't want me to be lonely.' After a few days she asked them, 'When will Harry be back? He said he'd be here all the time.'

They said, 'You know what he's like.' Jo didn't know what they meant.

She got a job in a pub and worked fourteen-hour

shifts. She sent photos from Hampton Court, from the Tate, from various castles. I asked why Harry wasn't in the photos. She said, 'Harry's busy. He's got his dissertation. It takes up a lot of his time. And it's a four-hour train ride. It's understandable if he can't come back all the time.'

I said, 'Didn't he tell you the train ride was one hour?'

During uni holidays Harry came home and they went ice-skating and made pizza. He took her to a party and she met his friends. He surprised her with a trip to Paris but sulked the whole trip because Jo didn't speak French. He took her to see Buckingham Palace and Jo slipped on the icy path. She lay on her back and laughed, holding out a hand for Harry to help her up, but his eyes were narrowed and he spoke to her through closed teeth. 'Get up,' he hissed. 'Stop embarrassing me,' and his eyes flitted nervously to the palace windows, as though the Queen herself might peer out and see his girlfriend sprawled on the path.

Later he told her he was planning a trip to Scotland with his friends next holiday and Jo couldn't come. He asked if while he was away she could keep up with current affairs so they'd be able to have more intelligent conversations. She called me that night and we drafted a break-up speech. We were careful with our language, sure to mention love and respect; we used reasons rather than excuses; we said something about growing apart, becoming different people. She called Harry, looked at her notes, and said, 'I've decided I hate you.' When she rang back to apologise he hung up on her.

Jo rang Dad and asked for money. She packed what she could fit in two suitcases, and Harry's mum drove her to the airport. By the time he came back and found her gone, she was on the other side of the world, getting ready for her third winter.

Turning for home

At eighteen years old, I stood in front of a portrait of the Queen, swore some kind of allegiance, and boarded a bus full of other army recruits. I was trying not to cry.

The bus took off from Brisbane and began the two-day drive to Wagga Wagga, a town on the edge of the Australian Outback that either froze or shimmered in the heat. The bus pulled into Kapooka, the site of our basic training. We stood in front of our bags in neat rows, arms clasped behind our backs, and I asked myself, 'What am I doing here?'

It wasn't long into basic training that I realised I didn't have a single one of the skills necessary to succeed there. I wasn't strong enough. I couldn't run fast enough, or for long enough. I couldn't shoot straight or read maps. I couldn't switch off my anxiety and be led into an unknown situation. I had to alter myself to fit in. I shaved my hair off, I changed the way I talked, and how I walked – but this was mostly because my boots were too small and I lost feeling in my toes a few weeks in.

Near the end of training, I was being mistaken for a man more and more often, and when I visited home after graduating my sisters were scared of me. Not only did I lose my softness, my sensitivity, I forgot how to make decisions and assess things for myself. Mum remembers that on one of these trips home she asked if I could take the bins out for her. She says the expression dropped off my face, and whatever I'd been occupied with fell from my hands. I walked to the bins like a zombie. When I came back she said, 'I was just asking. It wasn't an order.'

After basic training, I was posted to a naval base in a rural area of Melbourne. The pub on base was subsidised, and there was nothing else to do. I was so consistently hammered that to this day I'm not entirely sure where it was that we were living. I remember only that there was a train track and some kind of estuary. In Melbourne I met Amelia and her kind-of-boyfriend Sam, and we quickly became a trio. Amelia and I bonded because we were the only religious people we knew, and had both drifted far from the comfortable, secure faith we'd grown up in. I told Amelia a story from basic training that had been going around in my head. A few weeks in, I'd failed a fitness test and been sent to a rehab platoon. In the two weeks I spent there, I got to know Marcel. It turned out I'd gone to school with his brother. Marcel had already been in the rehab platoon for over a year after falling off the ropes in the obstacle course with his rifle slung over his back. He'd fallen straight onto the rifle, nearly breaking his back on the cocking handle.

Marcel had volunteered to be the duty student of the platoon, taking on the extra responsibility because it meant he was allowed to get up before reveille and read his Bible for half an hour. I tried to explain to Amelia, in a roundabout way, that I'd been jealous of Marcel – not for his freedom to read the Bible, but that he'd gone to the trouble of arranging the time for it. I wondered what I was missing, why I didn't care enough to do the same. Marcel had this thing. It was something unnameable. Let's call it X. It was an identifiable but intangible thing. It was a sort of energy about him, perhaps a kind of certainty. Whatever X was, he had it and I didn't.

Amelia and I knew we needed better self-control, but how are you supposed to exercise self-control if you don't already have self-control? We wanted to stop drinking so much, to stop making decisions that hurt us, to make it to the church on base every Sunday, or at least some Sundays. Just one Sunday.

Amelia invited Sam to church with us one weekend and he agreed, only because he knew Amelia wanted him to go, but when Sunday came around we were too hungover. I didn't knock on her door, she didn't knock on mine, so we kept sleeping. Amelia dragged herself to the mess later in the morning, and found Sam there, dressed nicely, on his way back from church. When she asked why he still went without us he said, 'Because I said I would.'

After three months in Melbourne – whichever part of Melbourne it was – we were posted to Townsville, along with Gallagher, a cook with jet-black hair that stuck straight up like Johnny Bravo's. Gallagher annoyed me at first, but he made me laugh, and I liked the attention I got from him. I knew I shouldn't be stringing him along, but he was there whenever Amelia and Sam were busy, and I didn't want to be alone.

The night we arrived in Townsville, Amelia and I were warned not to walk past the infantry barracks alone, then were given rooms in the artillery barracks, which didn't seem much safer. My belongings were being shipped by Defence and had been held up for about a month. They arrived the day after Sam had intercepted a man named – for some reason – Hairy, who'd been in our kitchen trying to rally the men who lived in my building to come to my room. As I unpacked my boxes, I was slowly processing the fact that Sam had possibly just saved my life, but might not be there next time. One of the tall packing boxes was designed to be a portable wardrobe, so my uniforms hung on a long, sharp metal bar that hung inside the box. When the boxes were unpacked and I was breaking them down to recycle, I pulled out the metal bar, weighed it in my hands, swung it around a few times to test its useability as a weapon, and stashed it under my bed. When the boxes were thrown out and my room set to rights, I practiced rolling off the bed and grabbing the bar.

Peta, someone we knew from the Melbourne base, was in town. We went out together, even though we had never been friends. Later that night I stumbled back to my room, vaguely aware that Gallagher was plodding along behind me. He followed me up the stairs into my barracks; he followed me onto my floor; and when I fell into bed he slipped in beside me. I asked what he was doing, already half asleep, the room spinning, spinning. He said Peta didn't have anywhere to stay, and that he'd lent her his bed. In whatever realm of my brain was still partly functional, I wondered why she hadn't been given a room on base. As I fell asleep, I felt his lips on my skin and his quiet voice whispering, 'Why don't you like me?'

I woke in the morning, hungover, with his leg hoisted across me in my tiny single bed. I untangled myself and trudged to the showers where I noticed a hickey on my neck, high enough that it would sit above the collar of my uniform. It looked like a dying star, too dark to be covered by foundation. Amelia suggested I put toothpaste under the foundation and together we did the best we could to cover it up. Of course, that morning our training session was swimming.

When the foundation washed off in the pool I was pulled out of training, screamed at by my corporal, told I had low morals, and charged with fraternisation. My punishment would be a fine taken directly out of my pay. While working in the kitchen, Gallagher was asked if he was 'fucking the tall girl', and it was quietly suggested to him that he not shit where he eats.

When I asked him why he did it, he shrugged his shoulders and looked at the floor. We both knew the answer. He was marking me.

People started asking if we were dating. I'd say no and he'd say yes. Every night his shadow would fill my door and there was nothing I could do to make him leave. He would talk, and touch me, and shake me awake when I fell asleep. I was so tired. Too tired to keep arguing with him, and even though I found him difficult to be around he was only annoying sometimes. He was easy to talk to, he was always there, and I never had to be alone. So when people asked if we were dating, I started to shrug my shoulders and say, 'I guess so.'

Eventually Gallagher was sent on a three-week exercise. Amelia, Sam and I decided to try a local Presbyterian church. We went to the night service, and rose to leave as soon as it ended, but the three people in front of us turned around to say hi, so we sat back down. We slotted easily into a friendship. Sophie and Jasper were engaged, Max was their good friend and Jasper's flatmate. For the next three weeks, we'd meet them for dinner before the night service. I wanted to be like them and belong to them. I wanted to have grown up with this group around me, so I'd have one unchanging group of people, like they'd had. I wanted them to influence me and tell me what to do. We found out Jasper had never been drunk, so Amelia, Sam and I took them to the Strand. I bought Max his first Jager bomb and watched his eyes widen in joy. Occasionally he'd go missing on those nights out and we'd find him at the bar downing Jager bombs by himself.

Jasper, despite our bad influence, had that mysterious thing I'd noticed with Marcel, the duty student; he had that X.

After the three weeks were up, I arrived home to find Gallagher waiting in my room. He came towards me, his arms out, and I involuntarily backed away from him, hitting the wall behind me. He saw this, his expression dropped, he stormed out, and I got one last night of sleeping alone.

I spent my weeks looking forward to Sunday dinner before church. Gallagher refused to come with us, and would be sulky and jealous when I got home. I'd invite him every week, desperately wanting him to come. I don't know what I expected. Perhaps some miraculous conversion would make him a different person. Maybe he'd start sleeping in his own room.

We argued about this one evening in the hallway of the barracks. He pointed to a bowl in the kitchen that was growing mould over the inch of cereal that had been left for weeks. He said, 'I think the universe is something like that, like a mouldy bowl in the kitchen, and the mould just grew and grew until it became life, became the whole world. So maybe God is just someone who didn't wash his dishes.' Casey, a cook we worked with, came out of his room during this argument that had started in laughter and become something else. Casey and I had beef. We were famous enemies. There was no particular reason for this, but we seemed to fight every time we spoke. As Gallagher and I argued I sensed Casey had paused behind me. Gallagher looked at Casey, then spun me around, pinning my arms behind my back. Before I could wonder what was happening, Casey squared up, punched me in the stomach, and walked into the kitchen. Gallagher released my arms and went back to my room.

The following week, Gallagher came to church with me, but said he wouldn't come to dinner and meet our friends, so we skipped it that week and arrived in time for the service. During the sermon the anger seemed to come off him in waves. In my memory I can almost see the air shimmering around him. He gripped my hand till the knuckles went white and crushed together. He squeezed tighter the more I tried to pull away. I wasn't listening to the sermon. I was mentally walking through each avenue in my life, looking for a way out. I wanted to be outside my body, free of him, free to find a way back to something I was so sure I used to have. I thought of that X. I wondered again what it was about Jasper and Marcel, the people who had that thing, whatever it was. If I were to ask them what it was I'd have to say, *There's something about you. You have something I want and I think if I had it I'd be happy and safe and free. No, I don't know what to call it. No, I can't describe it. Can you tell me what it is?*

After church, Gallagher sat on my bed and started taking his shoes off, and I asked him if he could sleep in his own room. He looked over his shoulder to my one small window.

'It's raining.'

Reaching under the bed, I pulled out the metal bar I'd stashed there, and raised it to shoulder height. 'Get out of my room.' He looked at me and laughed, but the smile was one that made me feel sick all the way to my bones. I raised the pole higher. 'I'll hit you.'

'No, you won't.' He didn't move so I swung it down and the flat side slumped against the meatiest part of his arm. Only softly. I didn't want to hurt him. I wanted him to know I'd do it, but he gripped his arm and cried out in pain.

'What the fuck?'

'Get out of my room.'

'But. It's. Raining. Are you going to make me walk in the rain?'

'It's 200 metres. You're in the army, mate. You can handle a bit of rain. Are you leaving or not?' I could see the emotions processing, flitting across his expression, settling finally into a look of defiance.

'No.'

So I swung again, and he held his arms up. 'Fine. Fine! I'm leaving. God, you're such a bitch.' He stood and shoved his feet back into his shoes. I put the bar on my chest of drawers and fell onto the bed, stretching out, luxuriating in the free space while he stomped towards the door. He stopped suddenly, his head turned, looking at the bar. When he picked it up and turned back to the bed, I curled my knees against my stomach and pulled my arms up to protect my head and wondered if he'd ever stop. There was a particular feeling I had as he brought the bar down on my legs and arms. For eleven years I've been trying to describe it to myself, but it isn't one feeling, it's several confused and strangely calm realisations. It was the anticipation of knowing how much each blow would hurt, and that I could do nothing but lie there and brace for each whomp of metal; it was being upset and hurt but simultaneously explaining away what was happening; it was knowing that no one was coming to help me. But that is far too actualised to be what I thought at the time. I didn't have those words, but only the feelings they're describing.

I'd put this episode down to him being too young to control himself, too hurt and angry. But a year later, when I saw photos of that time and of the months that followed, I realised he never hit me anywhere my bruises wouldn't be covered by my uniform. Not just my fatigues with their long sleeves. He knew the parameters of my PT uniform, where the short sleeves ended, even the tiny shorts that had shrunk in the wash. Even that night, he hadn't acted like someone in a fit of rage. He'd stood above me calmly, impassively, like when I'd seen him bashing biscuits for a cheesecake base.

The movement towards this incident was so slow, so confusing, that I barely noticed it happening. Earlier he'd helped me buy a dress for a party. He'd been so kind that day. He'd found different sizes and passed them over the changing room door, and told me how nice I looked. But on the night of the party he told me I looked like a slut and sulked over his beer. I didn't realise at the time, but he spoke to no one else. He didn't have a single friend. When a friend in the kitchens gave me a bracelet he'd bought at a market, Gallagher had asked to see it, and then thrown it against my mirror, smashing the glass beads to pieces. In each instance, he'd shrug and laugh, we'd fight, I'd apologise, he'd forgive me. I'd wish he'd give me a visible injury that I could tell someone about; something that would make things obvious to me, so I could call him what he was. Give me something more than little marks under my uniform. Give me a bruise people will ask about, for which I'll have no explanation other than to point to you. Don't laugh when you do it so I can't say you were only playing around. Break my arm, you coward.

To make it more confusing, he still made me laugh, I still looked for him when I found myself alone. I can't remember which nights I liked him and which nights I hated him. I've tried to remember the events of our four-month relationship and have found I can't quite pin down what happened and in which order. Nights are indistinguishable from each other, like the whole relationship was one long night. The memories conflate, passing before me like shadow puppets. Sometimes I wonder if I made the whole thing up.

A few weeks later, Max drove me back from church and asked how I was. I told him I didn't know. Something needed to change but I didn't know what or how, not with Gallagher there.

'So leave him,' said Max.

'I can't.'

'Why not?'

'He lives in the next building. Where would I go?'

The four of us had joined the army as part of their gap year programme, and our periods of service started expiring one after the other. Amelia's year expired first. She wanted to sign up for another three years but her parents were making her go to Bible college. Sam decided to stay on, but was sent on exercise and wouldn't get back before I left. Gallagher also decided to stay but was given a new posting. The day he left, I could tell he was trying to say he loved me. He kept looking at me, opening his mouth to speak, and then saying nothing. I had been sick – not just physically: I was sick of him always being there, touching me, looking at me mournfully like everything I said hurt him. I could barely turn my head to look at him. He sulked all morning, and when his taxi arrived he left without saying goodbye. I was surprised to find I missed him, and that I couldn't sleep alone. I was supposed to visit him later in the year to meet his family.

The army operates under a shame/honour culture. Honour is gained by competency, a well-ironed uniform and a crisp slouch hat, or getting a keyhole shot, where one bullet passes straight through the hole the previous one made. Shame comes from ineptitude, sickness, and complaining about injuries. An injury is fine if you bear it well, but mention it too many times or expect easy treatment and you're a malingerer – a chargeable offence. Casey once collapsed from heat exhaustion and never lived it down. Sam suffered through a whole exercise with glandular fever rather than face the shame of asking for leave to go to the medic tent. I was too embarrassed even to put milk in my coffee, and I learned to drink it black. We all participated in this, taking turns at shaming and being shamed. None of us were innocent. Because of this, I was sick for three weeks before finally leaving work to visit the medic. A nurse looked in my throat and told me I had the worst case of tonsillitis she'd ever seen. At this point it had been too painful to swallow for two weeks, and my veins were shrunken from dehydration. I lay on a bed with my arms out while two nurses worked on me, blowing every vein they found. Eventually they put a hand under each arm, led me to a car, and drove me to the hospital on base. I sat on a hard plastic seat while a new nurse knelt in front of me.

'Do you have plans for the holidays?'

I nodded. I spoke and my throat felt like it was ripping. 'I'm going home in three days.'

'OK, well, we're going to put you on a drip and start you on antibiotics. But once we do, you'll have to stay and finish the whole course. You better ring your mum and tell her you won't be home for Christmas.'

She left to find a bed for me, and I held my phone in my hands, trying to stop crying before I made the call. I leaned my head back against the wall, mouth open, trying not to swallow, and I prayed for the first time in months. I'd felt like God was unapproachable, that he didn't want to know me. That I'd strayed too far and couldn't find the way back. I could barely form a thought, so all I said in my tired head was, 'I need to go home. Help me get home.'

My throat seemed to expand, as if a rush of cold air had blown through it. I felt like I was waking from a deep sleep and had opened the curtains. I approached the reception nurse.

'When they come back, can you please tell them I'm fine now?' The nurse stared after me and I stepped through the doors into the blasting Townsville sunshine. I walked the twenty minutes back to my dorm, swinging my arms in the heat. Taking my phone out to my small deck, I rang Gallagher and told him I wouldn't be coming to see him, that we were done. He said, 'Good. I wanted to fuck other bitches anyway.' I laughed and said, 'OK, mate. Well, enjoy.' I ignored the apology texts that came in later that night.

By the end of my gap year I found I didn't know how to leave the army. I had ideas of going to university, and if I got a deployment to Afghanistan I'd earn enough money to study without a student loan. But I didn't feel ready for university yet, and had no idea what I'd study. My sergeant promised he could get me on a deployment and asked me to call on the weekend to discuss it. His wife picked up the phone and told me he was out of town, which seemed strange as he'd specifically asked me to ring. At work on Monday, I learned she'd hung up the phone and flown at him, asking who the woman was calling the house on the weekend, and how long it had been going on. He shook his head at me. 'I can't get you on the trip now. Imagine how it would look.'

I transferred to Reserves and was posted to an artillery battalion in Brisbane where I could still work full-time. Another deployment fell through, and then another, and then a cook from my unit was killed in Afghanistan and I started to question the purpose of this war, if we were being told the truth.

Being in the army had started to feel like I'd fallen down a well. I could see there was light and open air above me, but I couldn't see how to get out.

Towards the end of the year, in the space of a fortnight, another deployment fell through, a friend spread rumours about me and I lost my entire group of friends, my main drinking buddy was sent to military prison for being drunk on duty at 9am, and my new boyfriend threw a party to celebrate his promotion and didn't invite me. I threw loose clothes in my car and drove to my parents' house on the Gold Coast to look up universities on their computer. By this stage, I'd be a mature student, so to be accepted to study philosophy at the University of Sydney I'd need to sit an exam or have a diploma. I had no chance of passing an exam because I hadn't used my brain in two years, so I Googled diploma courses and found that most were two years long, except one: Moore College. The Bible college that Amelia's parents had sent her to.

To be accepted to Moore I had to complete an at-home exam, and I needed a reference from my pastor. The exam asked me to write about a favourite Christian work of nonfiction. I asked Dad what his favourite was and typed as he described it.

The first obstacle came when my pastor refused to write me a reference. He had also attended Moore. He met his wife, a fellow student, on the train into Sydney on the first day of class. They didn't kiss until their wedding day and got pregnant on their honeymoon.

Eventually he agreed to write the reference if I joined a weekly Bible study group and read *Basic Christianity*. I joined the Bible study but gave the book to a friend who expressed more interest in it than I did. My pastor wrote the reference, but sent it directly to admissions without showing me what it said.

It just so happened that the previous year, the Anglican Diocese, who funded Moore, had made some bad investments and been hit hard by the financial crisis. Rumour had it they were nearly bankrupt, meaning financial support for Moore had dried up and they were relying on donations from supporters, and student fees. Moore was taking anyone who applied.

Amelia picked me up from the airport in Sydney and drove me to Moore. She was doing Reserves on Tuesday nights and had arranged a place for me in her unit. She and Sam had broken up shortly after she left Townsville. She told me that on his final exercise, he'd been sitting in his tent and decided to become a Christian, quietly, and on his own. He just realised suddenly that he believed it. I turned my face away from her, watching the shops whizz by, blinking tears out of my eyes. How had he found it so easy?

I told her about Gallagher and she said, 'I had my suspicions. I should have said something. Me and you weren't good friends for each other. I'm ashamed of that part of my life.'

My first fortnight at Bible college was the longest I'd been sober in a year and a half. When I walked past the Newtown bars and the boozy smell wafted out, my stomach would clench and I'd miss the noise, and the feeling of my feet peeling off a sticky floor.

There's a language among Bible college students that I had to learn quickly. I adapted to a new sense of humour, and laughed along with jokes that required an in-depth theological knowledge to understand. I once overheard someone say, 'He believes in the Christus Victor theory of atonement, rather than penal substitutionary atonement, and I can't be with someone if we disagree at such a fundamental level.' I adapted to this culture in the same way I'd adapted to the army culture, and to

Australian culture, and would later adapt back to New Zealand culture. If there's anything I know how to do, it's pretending I belong.

I very quickly noticed people at college had that X that Jasper and Marcel had. That thing I couldn't name. Meanwhile, I felt like there was something in my throat I couldn't cough out: a dark shadow in me, filling me up. I walked through my days with the feeling of Gallagher's hands on me. I was a body full of bullet holes. I wanted someone to tell me what a Christian was but I was halfway through Bible college and it was too late to ask. I was supposed to already know.

At about the six-month mark, I was sitting in a Doctrine lecture. I barely passed Doctrine, and I hardly listened to the lecturer because I understood so little of what he was saying. I had no context or framework for understanding. But I suddenly tuned in when I realised he was talking about the Ark of the Covenant. Having spent my early childhood in Ethiopia, this was of personal interest to me.

He said, 'The Ark contained manna, Aaron's staff, and the stone tablets the Ten Commandments were written on. It was the dwelling place of God, and all who touched it unceremoniously fell down dead. It was kept in the Holy of Holies, the inner sanctum of the temple, behind a heavy veil as thick as your hand. Priests would enter the Holy of Holies with a rope around their waist in case they died, so someone could pull their body out without having to enter. But now, that veil is torn and you, you are the dwelling place of God. There is no temple now, there is only you.'

Something shifted in me. It was as if someone had taken a blindfold off my eyes and thrown water in my face. At the time, I didn't think of this moment as the point at which I became a Christian, only as the point when that dark shadow disappeared, when I started prying Gallagher's fingers off me, saying to his ghost, 'I am a body fit for God, and you cannot touch me.'

By the end of the year, I'd realised what that X was. It turned out that peace is a heavy feeling like a weighted blanket, like falling backwards onto a mattress, maybe like turning for home.

The patron saint of loneliness

2019. Paschal moon.

Whenever I'm spoken to this week, when something is asked of me, when someone brushes against me or sneezes too loudly, the nerves in my neck prick. In a week I'll be housesitting in Miramar, alone with a cat. I'll go to new cafés, and for long walks on the peninsula. I'll read in the sun with a coffee. Just one more week.

Waning gibbous moon. Jesus is in the garden of Gethsemane.

I pick up my new glasses from the optometrist; I clean my house and pack too many bags. Before everything closes, I go to the bank, the post office, Countdown. I buy Easter eggs for my sisters and we have dinner together. One is off to Hamilton, the other is walking the Tongariro Crossing. On the way to Miramar, my car starts making a strange noise and I turn the music up.

The cat wraps around my ankles as I let myself into the house. He wails while I make a cup of tea, waiting for me to settle and give him attention. I take my tea and book to the seat by the window to catch the last of the sun. It starts to rain and a silence comes down, like a dark cloud, like a curtain closing over a stage.

Blood moon. Good Friday.

This is fine. This is just that heavy feeling that hits in the moments after someone leaves, or when you find yourself suddenly alone and you have to adjust to the silence, when the air sort of zips up and draws everything into itself, like the seconds after the needle is pulled off a record.

I'll go for that walk soon, but first I'll watch an Avengers movie to fill the silence.

The movie is exactly what I need. That dark curtain starts to pull back. By the end I have my shoes on and a water bottle in my hand. I stand by the door. I take my shoes off. I put on another Avengers movie and let it play in the background while I crush my Easter eggs and make cookies out of them.

How many ways are there to be lonely? Sometimes I feel caught between subcultures, unable to fully participate in any, only to circle the edges. Sometimes it hits me how small this country is, and how far, how far away we are. Not only do I live in a small country, but in a small region within it. And I'm on the edge of that small region, a long drive from the city, alone at the outer corner of a pine forest. It would be so easy never to be seen again. I could be forgotten, not just by this small country, but by all of history. I'd be that blank line on a family tree that doesn't branch off.

When I lived in Sydney, at Bible college, I was surrounded by people all week, and I would seek out moments to be alone, but on weekends, the dorms would empty. I'd kneel on my bedroom floor, then I'd be sitting on it, then my head would touch the carpet. Felled like a tree. No one to help me back up. Only that silence and empty rooms that were losing the light.

And not everything that happens to us can be expressed. Some things exist separately from language, and that too is a kind of loneliness. I wonder if you could see stories on an X-ray, like a shadow on the lungs. That seems to be where they sit, heavy on the chest, these things I can't talk about. These poor companions. These unwanted gifts.

This is the day Jesus was stripped naked in front of a crowd, but we don't talk about that. Neither does he.

I have loved being alone. I have always sought it. The day I moved into the house I built for myself I had only a lamp and the walls weren't lined. I slept on the floor and thought, *Never forget this feeling. Never forget that you made this*. When I built my house, I built the ability to work part-time, and live alone, and spend my mornings drinking coffee on my deck, my deck that I built. A few weeks later, at my desk, I learned I'd won a writing prize and I wished there was someone there I could tell, and the absence of anyone bloomed inside me and I felt sick with it.

The cat has killed a bird and left the remains on the front doorstep: a beak, and some kind of glistening organ, the size and shape of a broad bean. It's after Passover, but there's blood on the door. He licks his paw, and looks to me for approval. I don't want him to touch me, so I lock him outside and put on *Thor*. It's a good thing there are so many of these movies. I stop pretending I'll do something when the movie ends and get the next one ready to go. I need to wash my hair, but it takes so long and I don't know how I'll bear the silence.

Still waning. That unnamed Saturday between the death and resurrection.

When businesses open again, I drive to a café to hear human voices. I sit in the corner with the paper and listen to the two girls at the next table. They talk too fast, like they're in *Gilmore Girls*, and their jokes sound like ones they've prepared earlier, and maybe rolled out a few times already. One of them has curly hair and beautiful grey eyes, and I think she's the kind of person who might write a list of conversation starters and look over them in the car before getting out. The grey-eyed girl is still eating but the other has finished. Grey-eyes says, 'Thanks for hanging out with me. I know I'm boring.' The other shakes her head and says, 'You're not boring. I mean it. You aren't.'

'No, it's OK. I know I am.'

This is hard to watch. Grey-eyes breaks off some of her cake, lifts it to her mouth, but pauses to stare out the window, watching a man tie his dog to a bollard. Finally, the cake goes in.

'Sorry, I'm such a slow eater. I know I am.'

'You aren't slow. It's fine.'

I have to leave. It's become unbearable. I'd rather be alone again than witness such a failure to connect; to watch someone try so hard and fall so short.

I park outside the house and stay in my car. Something in me heaves. I wonder how I'll fill all the years that are left. I project too far forward and see only loneliness for all my days. I can't take a deep breath.

Loneliness is a sickness in the blood. It's an amputated limb.

Easter Sunday. Mary looks for the body.

I go to church but leave halfway through. It's the funny thing about being lonely – it makes you draw away from people.

There is no patron saint of loneliness. I Googled it. Some have tried to make it Rita of Cascia, a woman who lost her whole family before the age of thirty-six, but she remains the patron of wounds, mothers, and marital problems, though they can all be types of loneliness. It's almost better like this. It's too perfect really, that we have no one even to pray to.

I'll make my own saint. Perhaps a whale drifting in a dark sea. Perhaps a body falling in the desert.

Little Women

On my twenty-fifth birthday, I left the house for a bottle of milk, and when I came back there was a package wrapped in cardboard leaning against my front door. I shook it, flipped it over, and saw the name of my ex-boyfriend in the sender details. Inside, I found a gilt-edged copy of *Little Women*, bound in white leather, a gold filigree pattern embossed on the front. It had the heft of a family Bible. When I saw what he'd given me, I hovered my thumb over his name in my contacts, wondering if I'd made a terrible mistake in ending things. He explained on the phone that he'd noticed every time I spoke about *Little Women* I put my hand over my heart and sighed deeply. He'd sat through the 1994 adaptation with my sisters, scrolling through his phone while we blubbed and sniffed, laughing at the same parts we laugh at every time, reciting the lines we knew so well. He'd planned to buy the book for me when we were together, and still wanted me to have it, even though we'd broken up before my birthday.

I don't remember who first put *Little Women* in my hands, but I remember reading it in bed at seven or eight years old, reading it on the lawn, and on the library bean bags, and in a tree – which was disappointingly uncomfortable, but Jo read in a tree so I stuck it out. I kept a list of words and phrases I didn't understand and would take it to my parents the next day. 'What does it mean to "put on airs"?'

Though I still have the first copy I read, I try not to open it anymore because the spine has broken away from the gum binding, and the pages could easily tear out. Last year I got *Little Women* as an audiobook for my long commute, but had to stop listening because I was getting to work with splotchy eyes from an hour of weeping in my car.

My sisters and I watched the 1994 adaptation so many times that we could recite the whole script and find a quote to fit all situations. When I cut my long hair one sister said, 'Your one beauty!' We won't walk past the limes in Countdown without saying, 'Are limes the fashion now?' Growing up, we would have long debates over who was which sister. Dijana thought she was Jo, which was absurd because obviously I was Jo and she was Beth. She maintained that I was Meg, which I was appalled by. No one wants to be Meg. The youngest of us is Amy through and through, though she also claims Jo. We eventually created composites and managed to end the debate forever. By the time we settled this, I was well into my late twenties.

Some stories you read and love, but then they go back on the shelf. Others, like *Little Women*, you consume again and again. You want to roll in the stories, to hang them over your shoulders like a coat, and let them travel with you through your life like a companion, like a sister.

There is something fascinating about the lives of sisters. We have the Mitfords and the Brontës, Marian Keyes' Walsh girls, and the dystopian surrealism of the Kardashians. The friendship between sisters is complicated and fractious. They also live in a kind of isolation; the world of sisters is private. Each set has its own language and games, and shared history. No one else is let in, we can only watch when allowed.

I have this feeling, which I'm sure many have, that *Little Women* belongs to me and my sisters. There's something painful about other people's enjoyment of it, because it's our thing and for so long we didn't realise other people even knew about it. It's been disconcerting to read of other writers, like Patti Smith and Simone de Beauvoir, identifying with Jo, and realising our private world with the March girls was shared with other people. Some unreasonable and reactive part of me wants people to acknowledge how important the story is to me personally before I give them permission to enjoy it. It's distressing to hear others talking about *Little Women*, because it's like they're talking about me without realising that I'm there and can hear them.

People have related to Jo as a writer, as a tomboy, or as someone who struggled with the confines of being a girl in the world. I wasn't a tomboy, and I had no literary ambitions except to be allowed to read in peace. It was the family unit that I related to. Like the Marches, my sisters and I were alone in the world. By the time the book found its way to me, I'd already stopped counting the times we'd moved houses, regions, and countries. I'd been uprooted from communities so many times that I'd lost any expectation that relationships would be permanent.

Before finding the book, I'd been living in an isolated village in the Ethiopian Highlands where there were no other English speakers. My best friend and I didn't share a common language and worked out our games with signs and charades. My concerns in those years were with sickness, the leopard in the backyard, the bowls of blood and beads that were left under the tyre swing we'd unknowingly hung from a sacred tree. And then suddenly I was back in New Zealand, being told off by grown-up women for wearing gumboots to school and clothes that had rips in them. When a classmate brought her pet rabbit to class, Dijana asked when she was going to eat it. Rather than rotating between the same two videos, as we were used to, suddenly we had TV with cartoons, and the Spice Girls, and people selling exercise machines. The only thing that remained unchanged by my shift between worlds was the fact I had a family.

The stories I read were a point of consistency. No matter how many times I returned to *Little Women*, it was always the same. In a way that I didn't have the language to express as a child, *Little Women* was more than a story, it was the house I grew up in. The March sisters, along with Anne Shirley, Heidi, and Milly-Molly-Mandy, linked hands above me, like a roof.

Like us, the March family didn't have the right clothes. They were barred from full participation in society because of their poverty and their strict morality. Only a few scenes in the book take place outside the family home, and when they do leave, disaster waits. Amy falls through the ice, Meg sells out at a ball, Beth catches scarlet fever, their father is injured in the war. The family home is a place of safety and sureness, a retreat from a world they don't quite fit into.

The Alcotts also moved house more than thirty times before *Little Women* was written, often to escape the debts their father had racked up. Although the book is based on Louisa Alcott's own life, these moves don't make an appearance in the story, but anyone who's grown up with the same instability might see it shimmering over the text in the restlessness, the uncertainty, the isolation that she maybe didn't mean to include but which worked its way in subliminally.

It had been five years since that copy had landed on my front doorstep, so I slid it off the bookshelf, smelled the first page, and started reading. I was struck by the simple elegance of the writing, the vitality of it. 'Beth's Secret' is devastatingly well written without becoming cloying or sentimental. The proposal scene rejects traditional tropes and manages to be funny, honest, and slightly disconcerting. This isn't just a relatable, fun story for girls. This is a beautiful work of art that shines for an adult as much as for a child. Not every children's book holds up upon rereading. I broke my own heart by going back to *Little House on the Prairie* and realising Pa was selfish, controlling, and neglectful. The book was so appallingly racist that I would never put it in the hands of a child. The Famous Five are a good time but literally everything is gendered. The Faraway Tree still slaps, but I appreciate it on a nostalgia level. It's fun, but that's all. *Little Women*, however, had layers that had aged with me, and that I could only relate to as an adult, like circles of meaning that had been waiting for me to come back and understand.

As a child I enjoyed the raucous joy of their games and plays, burning Meg's hair, creating newspapers, and befriending the boy next door. As an adult, I could hear Alcott speaking through Jo about her own struggles with identity and freedom. She famously wanted Jo to be a literary spinster as Alcott herself was, but her editors forced her to marry Jo off. She did so, but you can feel Jo kicking and screaming all the way. There is something distressing about her eventual conformity, as though underneath the resignation is a wild animal shrieking in a cage.

My mum reread it a few months later and said to me, 'I never realised this was a book about mothers.'

Alcott is quoted saying, 'I am more than half-persuaded that I am a man's soul put by some freak of nature into a woman's body . . . I have fallen in love with so many pretty girls and never once the least bit with any man.' Considering the time, this could have been as much about power and autonomy as gender or sexuality, but you sense that both Alcott and Jo struggled with something they didn't have words for – not just the destiny they were being pushed towards, but also the things they were supposed to want but didn't. Each sister has different desires; wealth, a family, and in Beth's case, more life. Each desire is presented as equal, except Jo's, which so closely mirrored Alcott's own, and was written as something to be overcome and left in childhood.

Little Women doesn't try to reason away the sadness of growing up. Jo says to Laurie, 'We can never be boy and girl again: the happy old times can't come back, and we mustn't expect it. We are man and woman now, with sober work to do, for playtime is over.' Jo is not Peter Pan, gathering fellow children and trapping them in infancy. Jo's resistance means she is left behind by her sisters. The noise and games of childhood wind slowly down, getting quieter and further away, until Jo finds herself in an empty room, suddenly so lonely that she reaches for something to lean on. This book is not wish fulfilment or fantasy. These are ordinary girls with ordinary lives, who grow into ordinary adults. But Alcott shows us the sparkling brilliance of ordinariness, and the simple potency of having a home and a family.

Mother of

I used to work in the office at a swimming school. One afternoon a young girl came to watch her sister's class. The girl cradled a swaddled baby, and stared lovingly at it while it slept. The girl must have been twelve at most. I wondered if the baby was a sibling. The parents were sitting in plastic chairs watching the lesson. I expected them to look back occasionally to check the girl wasn't carrying the baby wrong, wasn't about to drop it in the pool, but they didn't. There was something in the look on the girl's face that told me the baby was hers. She must have been the youngest mother I'd ever seen, but she was taking such good care of the baby, pacing behind the row of chairs, jiggling it slightly and whispering. *Some people are such natural mothers*, I thought. *Even at her age.* I walked past the seated parents some time later, and cast a glance at the young mother and her baby. There was a Wilhelm scream in my head as she turned and I saw the baby's plastic head.

As a child, my mother was devoted to her dolls. She

knitted dresses for them, and put them to sleep in a Sixties-pink cradle. When I was born she was thrilled to find that having a baby was like having a doll that moved and gurgled, that she could dress up in the clothes she made.

I never knew what to do with dolls. I carried them around because it was what other kids did, but they hung at my side, dangling by the ankle, hair trailing on the ground.

Something about the domestic ideal creeped me out, though I didn't have those words for what I felt. I watched ads for dolls that became closer and closer to real babies. One appeared to really drink from a bottle. There was even a toilet-training doll, who came with a doll-sized roll of toilet paper. The ad exclaimed excitedly that she 'really tinkled' when sitting on the doll toilet.

The only doll that amused me for any length of time was a Barbie with temperature-sensitive paint over her eyes, so that when I held a hot cloth against her face the eyes turned purple and appeared closed. Cold water would open them again. I entertained myself for a while, putting her to sleep and waking her up, but when the paint started to fade and the eyes glazed I cut her hair off.

At primary school, I'd sit in a circle of girls at recess and we'd plan our own families. I'd tell the circle I was going to have 'twin girls named Amber and Kristy', as though I could choose them from a vending machine when the time came.

In my early twenties, my friends began to have real children. I waited for a change to occur in me; something that would tell me it was my turn, that this was something I wanted now. I got older and nothing happened. There was only a silence in my body where there was supposed to be some maternal pull.

Many friends have said they were like me once, never thinking of children. They were sure it wasn't for them. But they woke one morning and, like an alarm had gone off, they knew it was their turn. They had to have a child as soon as they could. Now they're mothers. They carry packets of crackers and containers of sliced grapes. They have small bodies bouncing on their knees, and they tell other small bodies that it's bedtime. I ask them what age this change happened, when that alarm went off. They all say thirty. As I approached thirty, I didn't know what I feared more: the sound of that alarm, or the realisation that it wasn't coming, that I slept through. I'm afraid that my desires are out of my control, that I'm at the whim of a biological impulse to propagate the species.

I have a gold cross that's been passed through four generations of eldest daughters. The cross travelled with my great-grandmother from Croatia. She died young and the cross was passed to my grandma, who gave it to my mother, who gave it to me, telling me I could give it to my eldest daughter. The gold is paper thin, worn down by the four décolletages it has rested against.

At that point in my life, my career ambition was to

rescue children trapped in the sex trade. I was doing some work in this area already, but I wanted to do more than fundraising. I wanted to be in the field. I was going to devote my life to this work, but it was dangerous and I wouldn't be able to engage in it fully if I had children of my own. That was the first time I made a conscious decision about children: I would remain child-free in order to do the work I wanted to do, and, if the day came when I woke to find I wanted them, I would simply recognise the desire as a biological impulse and refuse. The decision was easy. The next morning, I hung our cross around my neck and thought, *Who will I give this to?*

Recently, I was having coffee with a friend, sitting at a table outside the café. A woman she knew from work walked past wearing a beautiful mid-length coat, the kind I've always wanted but could never afford. The rest of her clothes were Kowtow and her sneakers were that white white I can't maintain. My friend told me the woman and her partner decided not to have children, so they're always travelling and she can afford to dress entirely in Kowtow. I had to stop myself from asking, 'Why didn't they have children? What else do they do?' Because if you don't have children, you're supposed to do something else, as though there's a gap in all of us that must be plugged. Did she want to focus on her career? Does she have a dog? Because unmarried women have cats, and childfree women have dogs, didn't you know?

To suggest that we should replace the child-shaped gap implies that our lives are lacking. I don't feel a gap in me. I feel only that silence. So it's strange that I still had this thought about the woman with the coat. But the narratives we grow up in are difficult to shrug off, even when I feel myself to be living outside them.

Perhaps our belief in the gap comes from the idea that the purpose of our lives is to replicate ourselves. This is written into all of nature: the will to survive and reproduce, to scatter seeds in the wind and try again somewhere else. It's a biological, evolutionary impulse. If we refuse this role, do we have to make it up to humanity some other way, with work, or a pet? If I won't love a child, watch me love a dog.

But the world has changed. There are too many of us. A child will accumulate a lifetime of waste and plastic, filling up their own corner of the ocean. Maybe this silence in my body is also evolutionary. Maybe some of us have been chosen to limit the growth of the population so that we, as a species, can trip on a little further.

A woman once told me I didn't want children because I was selfish. We fought about it at the time. I was furious. My heart pumped and my chest turned splotchy and red under that gold cross. I told her she had no right to say that it was my duty to reproduce and that in failing to do so I was failing the human race. Now I see that she was right. I am selfish. I don't want to teach another person to read and drive, and watch them suffer through high school, worrying about who to sit with at lunch and finding a date for the school ball. I've done all that, and the thought of returning to it seems interminably boring. I don't want to be woken in the night.

Sometimes I think about my own childhood and realise how patient the adults around me were. I remember the day I learned that my mother's name was not Mum, but Lee. I called her Lee the whole long walk to school. 'What's for dinner, Lee?' 'What's your favourite colour, Lee?' She laughed patiently, as she did for my whole childhood, giving me a false sense of my own hilarity. Over the last few years I've been realising how many things from my childhood were for my benefit. I'd assumed Dad had his own quiet passions for hide-and-seek and listening to *Jungle Jam* tapes in the car. I wondered why Mum never did crafts anymore, like when we were children and she'd teach us how to make wrapping paper, and paint glass candlestick holders. And then I suddenly realised that she probably never liked crafts, and those activities had been for my benefit.

How much patience does it cost a parent to laugh at endless repetitive jokes, to read *Hop on Pop* over and over, to run through the house pretending you haven't seen a child in an obvious hiding spot? I don't think I have it in me.

I read Sheila Heti's *Motherhood*, a work of autofiction in which the narrator philosophises at length over whether to have children, aware that the window is closing and she has to decide. I thought I would relate more than I did, but the narrator's journey is different from mine. She seems to be deciding whether she wants a baby, whereas I'm sure I don't want one. I think I'm sure. The decision I have to make is whether I can accept that I don't want one. I'm worried I want the wrong thing. I don't want to want what I want. I'm supposed to want a child.

Heti writes, 'There is a kind of sadness in not wanting the things that give so many other people their life's meaning.' I'm afraid to step off the marked path. This place is not on the maps.

Emilie Pine, in 'From the Baby Years', an essay about her struggle to conceive, wrote that not having a child felt like a continued failure. I feel similarly, not about failing to have a child, but failing to want one. Every moment that I continue to not want a child feels like a failure against womanhood, against biology, against the things that were decided for me when a rush of hormones in the womb turned me into a female.

I'm worried that Present Me is stealing from Future Me, because one day I may find that all I want is a child, but it will be too late because Present Me didn't think. Present Me was too selfish.

There are many things I enjoy now that I'll pay for later, like eating too much sugar and not exercising, like reading my book when I'm supposed to be doing something else. When I have diabetes and osteoporosis, will I be able to forgive myself for doing the things that made me happy at the time, without a thought for Future Me?

In my early twenties, I started dating a friend after a year of 'will they/won't they'. Shortly after our second date, I became wildly depressed. It was bad timing. My thoughts went around and around, binding me tightly. I worried he'd think I was boring, or that we'd get married and run out of things to talk about. This was not my first relationship, but I'd never had these fears before. I confessed all this to him, knowing it was too early for that much honesty. I knew that when the fog cleared I'd regret what I'd done, so as I left his house that day I told myself, *Remember you did what you needed now, and forgive yourself in the future.* He broke up with me shortly after, and two weeks later met the woman he would marry and have a baby with. The friendship that had preceded our relationship fizzled out. I was sitting opposite him at a table when his engagement was announced by our mutual friend. I had to clink his stupid glass with mine and congratulate him, all the while dying of shame at the things I'd confessed to this man I now barely knew. But then I remembered what I'd decided that day, and I forgave myself.

If I end up old and childless, perhaps alone, perhaps lonely, will I be able to look back on Present Me and say, *You did what you needed. You're forgiven?* I've had to forgive myself for so many things. Will this one be beyond me?

When my friend Freya married her husband, they decided together that they didn't want children, but at 30 she woke to the sound of that alarm. She had a baby at 31. For years she tried to convince her husband to agree to a second. I ran into her on the street one day as she was hurrying back to her car, brushing away tears. Her voice shook and she hiccupped as she told me she'd just found out her window had closed. She would have no more children. I cried too, but I cried because my friend was sad, not because I understood the source of her grief. I searched for something that would help me know what my friend was feeling, but there was no concept I could relate to. I think I would have felt relieved not to have to decide. If the choice was taken away from me, I'd have nothing to forgive myself for.

Is it an insult to my friends who want children and can't have them, that I am fertile and choose to be childless? Fertile is a strange word for such a thing, as if I am good soil, the right pH balance, no stones in my field. Things can grow in me. What a waste to have good soil and not plant.

When I was sixteen my friend and I used to play a game. Now that I'm an adult it seems like such a dark game, but we had little understanding of what it is to suffer. We'd create increasingly dire scenarios for each other and would say whether, in that particular crisis, we'd get an abortion. I always said no. She'd mostly say no, except for situations involving her mother disowning her. My reason for consistently saying no was knowing that I could never be sure enough about my decision, and I'd probably remain unsure until the baby was born and it was too late. 'But anyway,' I said to her, 'you can't know until it happens to you.'

When I was nineteen I went to Magnetic Island. I was in the army at the time and my boyfriend had been posted to the other side of the country. I was sick and didn't have much energy, but I wanted a weekend alone. When I got to the island, a cyclone hit and the boats were cancelled. The electricity blew out. I couldn't leave the house, and I realised my period was late.

I rang work before my phone died to say I was stuck, then I lit candles and stood by the window, staring out into the black evening, thinking about my boyfriend and pressing the bruises he'd left on my body.

I knew immediately that if I was pregnant I wouldn't tell him about the child, even though at that point we hadn't actually broken up. I made a mental list of which mutual friends I'd have to ditch to prevent the news getting back to him. A child would tie me to him forever. I'd never be free, never be free.

I had a good job. I could support myself and a child. I could buy the baby tiny shoes and a tiny bucket hat. I could do school runs, and art classes, and sit in a deck chair at Saturday morning sports with the other parents. I could do it.

When the storm passed I caught a bus to the docks. The bus stopped at a traffic light next to the beach. I watched a woman putting sunscreen on her daughter's scrunched up face, and I thought, *Maybe I could even want this*. Then I imagined a baby with my boyfriend's sticky-uppy hair. I remembered how his hands had seemed to leave ashes on my skin. Suddenly I wanted to smash the bus window and push the shards into my uterus, just in case.

My first night back home I woke with cramps that felt like his fist in my kidneys. There was blood on the sheet, and I stared at it and thought of little shoes. I spent the night trying to find a way of lying that eased the cramps. I curled over my knees, head in my hands, and rocked back and forth. The positions of pain and relief are so alike.

At which point does a child come into existence? It feels like the moment I wonder about having one, an Idea Child is born, and is then snuffed out by my decision not to. If I didn't decide no, the Idea Child would grow to a real child, and one day I would look back on that moment of decision and think, *What if I'd decided not to have you?* I'd be so grateful, and I'd feel sick at how close I came to snuffing out the Idea Child. Heti writes of a friend who held her new baby and said, 'I can't believe I almost didn't do this.' Freya used to look at her son and think, 'I almost missed out on you.' She was so grateful and so relieved that she hadn't lost this baby by deciding not to have him.

At this point in my thinking, a parallel life starts to

grow up through the floor. I imagine myself forward from the point of decision. The floorboards break apart and reform in new places. The walls warp and extend, adding rooms onto the house – a bigger kitchen, a dining table. In this parallel life, I'm in my mid-forties. I'm wearing mum jeans unironically. A ten-year-old works on a dance routine with their friend. From my spot at the new table, I remember Present Me, sitting at my writing desk. The clock runs backwards, the house shrinks, the child resumes their place in my body, their status as Idea. I'm back at my desk thinking, I'm sorry Future Me, but I don't think I want that. You have to lose the child. You have to try to forgive me.

I wish I could ask the child, do you want to be born? Am I stealing from you? Exchanging your life for mine?

Before realising I had that silence in my body, when I assumed I would have those twin girls from the vending machine, I used to dream I had a baby but it was too small. It fit in the palm of my hand. Each time I looked it was smaller, till it had shrunk to the size of my finger. I put the baby in my pocket for safekeeping, but when I put my hand in the pocket, the baby was gone. My fingers poked through a hole in the fabric.

Thinking now of my friends who have children, it was the transfiguration that disturbed me the most: that a person can shift their identity so profoundly. One day you are one thing, the next you're something else. My friend Amanda once got so drunk she pissed herself at the races. Now, she says, 'Don't make me count to three,' in her Mum Voice. She knows things mothers know, like how long meat can be left in the fridge, and which medications to take. She shares a smoothie with her toddler, putting the sucked-on straw in her own mouth. Mothers had been a distant concept to us, something we possessed, not something we were. Mothers went into a corner and powered down when we were out of the room.

I don't believe I'll ever know these things that mums know. These things about patience and meat, and medications. I'm worried I can't love anyone. Not in ways that matter. I'm not saying I'm deficient. I'm good at other things.

When I worked at the swimming school, there was a box of spare goggles for kids who forgot theirs. My boss told me only to give out the pink ones. That way, the boys would refuse to wear them and the parents would buy a new pair. The boys would ask me if there was another colour. My boss would stick her head around the corner and I'd say that's all we had. The boys would say, 'Please. Please find another colour.' The parents would explain that it didn't matter but the boys would cry that they wanted to go home, that they couldn't be seen in pink goggles. The parents would say they paid a lot for lessons and they weren't going home. The boys screamed and spluttered, their mouths wide, their eyes wild and desperate. They'd say, 'Please, please don't make me.' I felt their cries grip around my heart. I tried not to cry myself. If my boss left her desk, I'd sneak the boys green goggles and ask them not to tell. Then I'd return to my desk and consider what that feeling was, that grief when a child was unhappy. Is this maternal? Is this biological? Does this mean the silence in my body is not total?

Convince me to choose something else. I don't want to make a mistake. Part of me hopes that I'll fall in love with someone who'll desperately want a child, and I can give him one as a gift. I'll say, 'I made this for you', and it will be OK because he was sure what he wanted and I was not. That way, whatever life I find myself in, I won't be the one to blame.

The thing I finally admit is that I don't trust myself to decide. I want to give up the choice. Push me around. Tell me what to do. Let me quietly run out of time.

Only the lonely

Of course it would go like this. I finally meet someone who's actually nice to me, and the whole nation gets sent to their rooms.

I knew you were trying to talk to me, but at first I thought you were weird. The death toll was creeping up, but soon I was barely noticing because all I cared about was how blue your eyes had seemed when I took my cup to the kitchen, and you looked up at me from the dishwasher and said my dress was pretty. I said to my friends, I can NOT self-isolate right now.

Later, I wondered if you'd stand next to me while everyone in the office watched the 1pm briefing. I thought: if we stand at the back of the kitchen, maybe you'll find a way to secretly touch my arm, or tap a hand quickly against the small of my back. It had been so long since I let anyone touch me. I didn't remember the last time.

On the day the lockdown was announced, you asked when I was leaving work. I said, 'As soon as I figure out which of these cords is the laptop charger.' You asked me to wait, and walked with me to the train. Leaves were scattering across the road, and people in suits walked against the wind, carrying computers and pot plants. You said, 'It's going to be so long before I see you again.'

As my train arrived, I asked you what the rules were for saying goodbye, because you're so weird about PDA, and I still didn't know what we were allowed to do. I held out my hand for a fist bump, and you laughed and kissed me. You'd never done anything so public, and I didn't want to leave yet.

You drove forty minutes to see me, past police setting up roadblocks. You couldn't find my house in the dark, and your flatmates were texting asking where you were, saying they were going to lock you out if you weren't back by the time Level 4 started at midnight. We were never going to have enough time. I was hearing stories about people quarantining with someone they'd just started dating so they wouldn't be separated for so long. I wondered if you'd suggest it, but my house is too small, and I knew the only thing worse than isolating alone would be isolating with someone else's flatmates. I planned how I'd say no in a way that wouldn't make you feel rejected. But then you had to go, and our time was up. I walked you to your car and thought, *Ask me. Ask me.*

It's five minutes past midnight and I'm three whiskies in and I'm pacing my small kitchen. I can't believe you left. While putting your shoes on that night, you'd asked if I'd ever write about you. I said, 'Not unless you do something wrong', but the next day I started this. It needed an ending, and I knew I'd never finish it because there would be no end for us. I knew when you looked up from the dishwasher and said my dress was pretty. I'd really looked at you, after all those months of thinking you were weird, and a little voice in my head said, 'This is it.' I'd never done that before. It's not what I do.

My grandpa tells me he remembers quarantining during the Spanish Flu. I think he's forgotten that happened after WWI, not WWII. I don't know if he means to lie, or if he creates stories in his head and believes them. I can't judge because I do that too. There are so few stories of the Spanish Flu. It's like no one wrote anything down. I want to capture everything about this. I want to be able to describe it in forty years. I'll tell people how my whole street smelled like pot, and how the only beer left on the shelves was Corona. And the memes. So many memes. I imagine what we'll all do that first day out, and what the world will be like afterwards. I would be perfectly happy with this, if only you were here and we could talk about everything that is happening and not happening.

.

We text about our days. We video call on your lunch breaks. You still have work to do, but I can't do much from home. You're with flatmates. I'm alone. We talk we talk. I learn what times of the day you're free and adjust my routine. I send photos from my walks. You send photos of your view. You tell me at night that you're thinking of me, and I ask you to tell me what you're thinking. There's something blissful about how much I miss you, about how I can't concentrate on anything else but counting down the days, and wondering when my phone will light up. You're not the best at texting, and people who can't text have no business getting into relationships, but you're doing the best you can, and I structure my days around waiting for you.

.

The lockdown has been extended. I don't care about anything else now. I don't care about recording events. I don't care about the new world order or the socialist paradise that might come from this. I don't want to read the Arundhati Roy piece that I saved, or the Covid novel that Ali Smith is definitely writing. I don't want to write a 'Love in the Time of Corona' essay. Representations of life aren't enough anymore. Give me the real thing or burn it all down. I only want to show up at your door, and for you to do the things you say you'll do. I want you to kiss me in the elevator at work, or press your body against mine outside a restaurant like you did that time, when your hands slid up my shirt and you breathed against my neck. The imprint of you is fading. My arms close around empty air.

You're often late for video chats these days. Today you cancelled and I washed my makeup off and felt stupid that I'd wasted all morning waiting, but what else is there to do?

.

You're allowed to go into the office in Level 3, and I wish I could go in with you and circle you in the kitchen, pretending for the others that there's nothing going on. You send a photo of my empty desk, but then I don't hear from you all day. You tell me later you had to work till 7.30, but you send a picture of the sunset that you took when you left. It's full dark by six these days, but I don't think about that.

It was your birthday yesterday. I couldn't do much, but I bought a cupcake and put a candle on it. I sent a photo of it and wrote, 'Make a wish!'
And then I waited. And I waited.

.

Today I said you don't have to text me anymore. We both know you weren't going to, but this way I'm free from wondering. Something has changed, but you can tell me what it is later, when we start putting things back together. We'll be getting out soon. I don't want to video call, I don't want you to write. I'm tired of half-measures.

.

When I see you again, it isn't how I thought it would be. I thought maybe you'd jog a little to reach me quicker. I'd run my hand through that quarantine beard, and you'd wrap an arm around my waist.

I'd asked you when you wanted to meet because I was scared you wouldn't ask me and I didn't want to know that I was right. You'd said it'd be good to catch up and I sent a screenshot to all my friends to analyse the possible hidden meaning behind that particular choice of words. The general agreement was that I was overthinking. I knew I was.

You greet me with a hug and a pat on the back and I think, *Aren't we past hugging?* That's the only time you touch me. We don't talk like we used to and you aren't like you used to be. You are someone new and I don't like you like this. You talk for a surprisingly long time about council bins, and we argue about the monarchy. After an hour you say you have to go because people are coming over for a barbecue, but it's raining, and if I were having a barbecue, I'd want you there with me. I was going to wait until we were at your car, then I'd ask if you're OK, if I'd done something wrong, if

I'd misunderstood, or if there was another you – a you who'd been so nice to me but was gone now, and, if so, where did he go and do you have a map to that place? I have the words ready but you get in the car so quickly there's no time for me to speak. You say, 'I'll text you', and I know you won't. I know I've just gotten the ending of the essay I started writing about you. Whatever this thing was that we never got time to name, it's done.

I go back to the house I've been shut in for two months. I was here the first time you called and I was too nervous to answer, and when you first wrote, 'I wish you weren't so far away', and when you said it'd be nice to catch up. We've done one full revolution, and yet here I still am. I've not moved from this spot.

That wasn't worth the petrol it took to drive to you. It wasn't worth the half-hour it took to curl my hair. I wish I could pinch off the mascara I'm wearing and put it back in the tube, scrape the gel from my eyebrows. I want back everything I wasted on you.

I go back to work, but you're now in an office across the road and I can't decide what I'll do if I see you in the street. I could ask what happened, but you might say that you just stopped thinking about me and that would hurt too much, because I'm still thinking about you. I could say you disappointed me but I'll forgive you because you also made me happy for a while and sometimes that's all you get. Later I think no, not that.

Then I realised you'd visited the office, and you'd gone the long way to the printer because the short way meant going past my desk. I'm so mad at you for making me cry in the bathroom. I'm mad because I want you to be in the kitchen making tea, and I want you to avoid meeting my eyes like you used to because people might see what was going on. They might get zapped by the energy that was zinging between us. I'm mad because I think my friends are bored of hearing how mad I am, and because I thought you were better than me. I thought I was the lucky one, that someone like you would want someone like me, but I would never do what you've done, so I'm better – I'm the better one – and you're going to break *my* heart? I'm mad because it's embarrassing how much I wrote about you in my journal, like I'm literally embarrassed in front of my journal. I even apologised in the pages, but if there was more to write I would write it. At the end of the day, you're waiting at the traffic lights on the other side of the road. You smile awkwardly. I ignore you as we pass each other.

My colleagues are speaking to me, but I don't hear what they're saying because I'm thinking how badly I want to clutch my chest and tip off my chair, like I'm having a heart attack. I want to howl about how awful you were, and how much I wish you were still being awful because at least then you'd be here. But you're not here. You aren't looking at me. I should be able to call an ambulance for this feeling, like I should have been able to call you but never did, even before, because I wasn't sure you'd answer.

There are things I could do. I could play *Animal Crossing* like everyone else. I could re-watch *Schitt's Creek*, but I don't want to be distracted from this feeling. I want to nurture it, hold it close, because it's all you left me when you left me. It's the only thing I want to talk about. You've made me selfish. I talk to my ex and he's mad at you, too. I say to him, 'I'm so sorry if I ever made you feel like this.' He tells me it's OK because it passes, like everything passes, like how the good part of this passed.

I have to unlearn the habit of telling you everything, like the funny things that have happened at work, and what it's like being back without you, and how sad it is going to the kitchen and not finding you there. I can see your new building from my window. They're doing renovations and I wonder if the noise bothers you, and if you stop yourself from telling me about it.

I don't want to finish writing this because it's the last thing to do. I should unfriend you on Facebook – I should get in first – but it seems like too quiet an end.

Ah, it's all right. It's all all right. I just miss you, the you that you were before. We would have been perfect if you weren't the way that you are, if we were both other people.

Easy to love

I went into lockdown a hardcore introvert, smugly planning how many books I'd read and how much bread I'd bake. I emerged two months later, having spent my idyllic evenings weeping audibly on the kitchen floor, desperate for interaction, hollowed out by loneliness.

Afterwards, I couldn't fill my time with enough people. No matter how much I crammed in, that moment still came when someone would say, 'Oh well, better let you go', and I'd want to reply, 'Don't let me go. Don't ever leave. Come live with me in the bush in my tiny house.' At the end of each day, I was alone. The desperation was coming off me in waves. I was afraid of my own company. So, I finally did the thing I'd been putting off for years. I downloaded Bumble.

My dating history has mainly been periods of high activity between long recoveries. I make terrible decisions. I'm attracted to dismissive men who can't text, people who forget to tell me they are married, or gay. I always think I want to be loved and adored, and when I get that I feel suffocated by it. I once had a date duck into a dairy to buy a porn magazine and ask if he could put it in my bag. He later assaulted me. By twenty-three I felt old and jaded, worried my ultimate turn-off was being liked back. When a year-long relationship ended I decided to take a break from dating. I moved to New Zealand, built a tiny house, got two degrees, wrote a book then threw it out and wrote another one. Suddenly it had been eight years and I still couldn't bear the thought of getting back in the game. I'd believed the Buzzfeed articles about the kinds of messages men send women, and thought as soon as I looked at a dating app I'd be batting away dick pics and requests for nudes.

But then, just before lockdown, I'd suddenly realised all the men in my life are actually cool, and maybe I didn't need to be so scared of them. So I did the sensible thing and dove head first into a three-month situationship with a co-worker. Every time he sent a photo I was scared this one would be the dick pic. It was often just a view of the harbour from his deck. You might say it was a deck pic. Just as I started to feel safe, like maybe I'd found a good one, he ghosted me and I thought I'd never get over it.

The grief wasn't really over him. I barely knew him. It was more that he had lifted me out of my isolation long enough for me to see how alone I'd been, moments before dropping me back in it. It wasn't that I missed talking to him, it was that I now recognised my endless days as a gaping silence, and that silence rang in my ears like tinnitus.

I started swiping through photos of men holding fish. I matched with a few people who gave off safe vibes but was too scared to talk to them, so my friend Joan came over for coffee and moral support. We picked two matches and spent twenty minutes coming up with 'Hey, how's your weekend going?' The first to reply told me he'd been 'working on some documents'. I wrote several iterations of 'What am I supposed to do with that information?' before backspacing and unmatching. The second was a very nice Canadian who for the purposes of this essay we will call Canada. Canada and I got coffee after work. He had a 10/10 beard. He was interesting and a little sad, and I enjoyed our conversation even though he didn't ask me a single question. When I checked my phone on the train home, my friends were in a chat group timing how long the date had been, surmising after a few hours that it must be going well. I told the friend committee that it had been fun but I didn't particularly need to see him again. After the requisite two to three days, Canada texted to say he was sorry for being weird and rambly. He'd been nervous. He didn't date very often. He was nervous? I hadn't been able to pick up my coffee because my hands were shaking. I'd assumed I was one of many women he'd been talking to, that he was rushing off to dates every week and wouldn't miss me if I never texted again. I typed and deleted several times, 'Hey, you want to be friends?' I asked the friend committee, all more prolific daters, if that was an OK thing to say. The committee decided it was a little weird, and would be an impossible friendship to maintain. I figured that now I was a 'casual dater' I couldn't go around making *friends*. Besides, I had another date lined up that night. I didn't send the message.

The second date was American. We talked about morality, religion, whether perfection is possible, the dot in the yin–yang symbol, and whether we'd renounce our beliefs to save our own lives. A brief glance at my phone showed the committee saying, 'It's been four hours!' I texted America a few days later, having decided not to confer with them this time, but to do what felt right to me: 'Hey, you want to be friends?'

I started asking everyone I met about their experiences of dating over apps – even people I was on dates with. I had come to this late and felt like the new kid at school, trying to catch up on the social dynamics to find where I fit. The last time I was actively dating, there were no apps. I met people by walking into a new workplace/church/class and thinking, 'Right. Who should I fall in love with?' I wanted to know the average user's experience. How many matches was normal? How many conversations do you have going at one time? How many dates do you go on before having 'the conversation'? The average users all seemed to agree that dating on apps leads to a kind of misanthropy, and tired resignation: you suffer through multiple awkward dates, you try so hard, and nothing ever works.

By that time, I'd gone out with a Kiwi, would have happily met up with a Croatian had he not turned out to be my friend's brother, and finally delved into second-date territory with an Aussie. In three weeks, I'd been on more dates than Canada had been on in two years. I couldn't reconcile my experiences with the ones I was hearing about. I'd not been sent a single dick pic or abusive message. I'd had so much fun with each person. Was this not normal? Where were the awkwardness and the disappointment and the crying on the way home? I could barely remember what I'd been so afraid of. I wanted to ask my dates if they were tired of this, if they'd had to drag themselves out to meet me, and if they'd go home feeling, once again, like there was no one out there. I also wanted to say, 'I don't feel that way, I'm not nervous anymore, and I kind of love you.'

Maybe it was just that I was new to this and it was still shiny to me. Or maybe it's that everyone is smart and interesting.

Dating columns too seem peppered with despair. Sometimes I could sense that despair, at the edges of my vision, when I wondered if anything would stick, or if I'd ever learn to like what's good for me. And sometimes I worried that dating is unsustainable for me because I'm so deeply attached to everyone I've been on dates with, even if I haven't seen them again. I hate the idea that I might be another sad Friday night to someone, just a picture in an app of someone whose name they can't quite remember. If I've been on a date with someone, they're memorable to me. I still see and talk to many of them, and regularly wondered, months on, if it wasn't too late to message Canada to see if he wanted to be friends.

The ghoster who started all this walked past me in the street yesterday. I kept my eyes forward and breezed past, flicking my hair, high-fiving myself for being a strong female character. But really, I wanted to run back, to shake his shoulders and say, 'You know me! I've had pictures of you in my phone. You've been to my house, and you're just going to walk past?' But I also want not to yell. I want to forget that he hurt me, and ask how his flatmates are, and if he still has to work those crazy hours, and if his sister got that house. I hate the idea of moving backwards from any level of intimacy, so I would forget everything he did, wipe the slate clean, for one more moment of friendship.

If I could say anything to the ghoster, I'd say that I'd needed for us to work because I thought there was no one else, but I was wrong. There are so many lovely people, and I've been so lucky to meet the ones I have, and I haven't yet reached the bottom of the barrel. Everyone is so easy to love.

Dating is such a generous thing, it's such a kindness that people want to meet and listen to each other for a few hours. I want to know everyone, I want to know what you're obsessed with, and how you got that scar. Tell me about your family. Fill me up with stories. Let me make you laugh.

ii

I'm obsessed with love. All forms fascinate me: familial love, aromantic love, queer love, longing, friendship. But my interest has come from a position of anthropological curiosity. In my own life, I've been reasonably love-averse. I'm not into romantic gestures. I don't have a secret wedding Pinterest board. The only time I've tested my name against someone else's was when talking to someone on Hinge whose last name was Smellie, and I realised I could marry him for lols and become Alie Smellie. I think I've been afraid of love. Maybe in the same way I'm scared of any extreme thing, like huge bodies of water, or driving too fast, like it's too bright or too loud.

I've always felt that loving someone means giving them a certain amount of power over you, so I've held myself back from it. My ability to move on from each relationship has depended on how much power I gave away, and how much I could take back at the end. By this I mean, how much did I let my feelings show, and was I able to get a refund on that affection and pretend I never cared.

Then I listened to a podcast which featured a line from an Auden poem: 'If equal affection cannot be, let the more loving one be me.' I had to pause the podcast and sit down. What a thing: to consciously choose to love more, to actively seek it. It's so bloody lovely. This would look like not worrying about texting first, or replying too quickly. It would mean letting someone know you like them without fear or embarrassment. I looked at the world, and the relationships I'd been in or witnessed, and thought: how different would it be if we were in competition to love each other more? To meet the love we receive and give it back ten-fold. *What if next time*, I thought, *I just gave all my power away and loved openly and affectionately? What if I let someone fully in?*

This all happened some time in January. The last days before Covid. I was about to meet the ghoster and begin my dating rampage, and you already know what happened. I went all in, and I got my heart broken, more than once. Of course I did. It was always going to happen, because this isn't some prosperity gospel where you get out what you put in. But I didn't do it to get anything from being the more loving one, but because it was the kind of person I wanted to be: someone who loves freely, without insecurity or tit-for-tat power plays. I didn't want to give love to get love. I wanted to give it without expecting anything in return.

Today I stood next to the ghoster at the traffic lights, neither of us acknowledging each other, and I knew I'd rather have been the more loving one in that situation, because being a loving person means I'd rather be heartbroken myself than make anyone feel the way he made me feel. No question. Let me love you more, if only so I know I'm able to love; that I can pour it out; that if I need to, I can absorb heartbreak into myself and end it there.

204

I'm finishing this essay in my new boyfriend's living room – a boyfriend I hadn't met when I started writing it. We've met each other's families. I keep a toothbrush and a packet of hair ties at his house. I finally get good morning texts and bi-weekly dates. That's all I wanted. But we're at a point in our relationship that terrifies me, because I've never been here before. It's that last moment in the trust fall where you can stop yourself tipping over. I could expose my soft underbelly at the moment of most vulnerability, or I could snap closed. I want to be someone who can go into this without holding anything back and protecting myself, but sometimes I feel like a raw nerve.

And now, having written this, I'm realising how wrong I've been. Love shouldn't be bound up with power. Relationships shouldn't feel like a competition.

I don't want either myself or him to be the more loving one. I want only to know that I'm capable of love. That I can give and receive it without insecurity. I thought I should be able to give love without expecting anything back, but I was wrong. We all just want to be loved, right? It's why we're scrolling through apps, putting ourselves through this.

It's OK to want to be loved. It's OK to be hurt sometimes. You won't die. I promise. Give love anyway. Put more of it in circulation. Ask for some back.

How to write about God

Ask a lot of questions. Don't say what you know. Have only doubts. (Well, I have plenty of those.) Know that you know nothing. Know nothing but that.

Know that you could be wrong. (Oh, I know.) Know that to be wrong would be the worst, the worst.

Know nothing, but know this so surely: that I had to pick something; that I couldn't bear uncertainty. Couldn't find another explanation for that infinite regression of everything coming from something else, knew that behind it all there must be something uncreated, someone to tip the first domino. I cannot not believe there is a god. I tried. One hot Sydney evening, as I walked to the bus stop, I took off my belief, layer by layer, like items of clothing, tossing them behind me. My faith fell off me in waves. And when it was all gone I found, underneath it, nothing but more faith, an infinite reserve, so that by the time I reached the bus stop I knew nothing but this one thing: that I cannot not believe there is a god.

Write how believing there is a god is one thing. Liking him is another. And liking you, the church, well.

I keep trying though. I keep getting out of bed on Sunday mornings and, when you ask about my weekend, I edit myself so you won't look at me like that. I don't tell you about him, or that I came here from his house.

I don't want to explain him to you. I thought I wouldn't have to explain, but you keep sitting me down; you keep bringing me a record of wrongs. So go on, show me where it says I have to go before a priest, where it says I need a ceremony to perform this love for you. I'll show you how bodies are made into one, how a man cleaves to his wife. I have had enough of you. Get my name out of your mouth.

But again, I get up on a Sunday morning. I keep getting up. I keep driving home again covered in the way you looked at me. I drive home to that warm body, still asleep. Next week I will do the same, because it's written that I should, because God loves you, Church. He married you. So I keep asking him to help me love you too.

I also know you mean well. I know that, that time at Bible college, in the dining hall, when you said my clothes were wet and you asked me so nicely to change and come back, that it was out of concern for those men. All those nice men who don't watch *Game of Thrones*, who fast forward sex scenes, who are trying so hard. And I don't want to make anything harder for anyone who's really trying, but come on man. I just went for a swim. I just stayed too long and ran out of time to change, and my hair dripped down my back, and I had wet boob patches on the shirt I'd thrown over my bikini, and I'd thought maybe it would be better just to wet the whole shirt.

I didn't come back of course. I ate in my room and cried softly onto my wet shirt. And it was so sad, because when I'd been at the beach I'd thought, *God, how beautiful.* And I'd thought, *Who made the world?* And I'd thought, *All this is for me?* The sun had shot bright pink over the clouds, and I'd thought, *This is why I keep trying.*

I just want to be loved by you. I just want you to swing your arms wide and press my body to yours, though my clothes are wet. But you won't do this, so I'm alone with God. And what frightens me about Heaven isn't just the foreverness of it, but that you'll be there too.

Write about the good bits, like having something sure, having such a bright light by which to see. And like when our conversations pull out something new, something so complex and gorgeous we say Wow. Oh, wow. And when you ask what I'd like prayer for and I cry and cry and it's OK because next week will be your turn. And you say I know, I know it's hard. And I say, but isn't it good though; aren't we so glad to have this? And you say yes, oh yes. And like the times when we've left frozen meals on each other's doorsteps, and stuffed envelopes of money in each other's pockets, because what's mine is yours, and because you need it now, but I'll need it later. Or that time I snuck in late with my cousin, because we thought we ought to, and the pastor talked about not drinking foolishly, and we looked each other, sick as hell and still a little drunk, and nodded like, 'Yeah, fair', and we laughed and snuck back out.

Sometimes I think of the church in Sydney that burned down, some problem with the toaster. The congregation stood in the street and watched it burn, and then realised all together that the church wasn't in there. It was out on the pavement, quiet for once, shirts pulled over noses so as not to breathe smoke. So this is where I find you. Not inside walls. This heart lives outside its body. No fire burns you.

After the fire you put a sign over the crumbled, scorched bricks, saying 'New building coming soon', and someone graffitied on it 'That's what you said about Jesus', and we all thought that was quite good.

This is why I can't write about God without writing about you.

Even when you sit me down and ask me to explain why I do the things I do, why I won't just be like you, I can see how much you don't want to do this. I can see you hope I'll forgive you, and I will. Even though, when I see you, I'll have the feeling of sirens on the highway, wondering if they're coming for me.

But not everything that hurts is bad for us, and not

everything that's bad for us hurts. I'll forgive you because I know that this is how you love, and because you're just trying to do the right thing, and isn't that all we ever want? Just to do the right thing?

Write about trying to do the right thing; how it's the trying that really matters. Write about that theology: how at the end of it all, the end of beaches and wet clothes and wedding rings, it'll only matter that we kept trying.

Write about worship. Write how all of this is worship.

Good girl

It was one of those groups you join in your first semester of university, when you're still excited about new stationery and the thrill of hearing professors swear in class. I don't remember what manner of group it was, perhaps some social justice thing, or a philosophy club. I've never been able to reach back to the enthusiasm I'd had in those days, so happy to be a joiner. Whoever these people were, we'd had dinner in a cheap Thai restaurant. We'd gotten louder and louder, excited by whatever thing it was that had bonded us, that we loved enough to join a club of others who also loved that thing, but which I can no longer remember. I spent most of the time talking to the boy opposite me. All I remember of him was his curly brown hair, the ringlets somehow holding together even as he raked his fingers through them.

After the complicated ritual of a large group trying to split a bill with cash, we wandered down to a café for gelato. I stood next to the curly haired boy at the display cabinet. He had plenty of room to cross behind me to see the flavours on the other side, but, as he passed, he put his hands on my waist, as though we were crammed into a tight space. I tipped forward against the glass and righted myself. I don't remember what gelato I chose, or if I chose at all. I remember conversation sliding past me as I sat quietly, away from the boy – confused, mostly, about a feeling in my body, like a cold fist had reached through me.

I was the first to leave and when I got back to my small room I stood with my arms wrapped around my body, wanting to understand this much too dramatic reaction, wanting to go back and ask the boy: *Who are you to put your hands on me?*

Among my friends, I'm famous for not wanting to be touched. My friend Joan once held her arms out to congratulate me for something and then pulled them back, hands up, saying, 'Sorry, I forgot. I'm giving you a not-hug.' In a strange way, I was . . . touched.

After I handed in my MA thesis – I'd been spending ten hours a day hunched at my desk – I could barely turn my head, and my back was spasming. I had a voucher for one of the cheap massage places at the mall that I hadn't used because the idea of paying someone to touch me felt seedy. But I knew I needed to.

The voucher was for a shop in the busiest part of the mall. I walked past several times, casting my head about for anyone who might recognise me, as though I was walking into a sex shop. Finally, I darted inside and was told to wait on a plastic seat in full view of the shoppers passing by. I hid my face behind my hair and stared intently at my phone until a masseuse finally ended my humiliation and invited me in.

I still remember a girl in high school walking past me in a crowd and touching my hip. I remember a boss checking my work, questioning something, then saying, 'No, you're right' and grazing my arm with the back of his knuckles. The glances of our bodies together were so light, so insignificant, that I assume the touchers not only don't remember but would barely have registered the moment as it happened. Yet I've remembered those touches all this time. Those people meant something different to me post-touch than they did pre-touch. It's not that I hate being touched. It's that it's too intense. It's too intimate. It's an act of love by someone whose name I might not remember.

There have been times when I've looked back through my days, trying to remember the last time someone touched me; significantly touched me, like they meant it, like when someone puts a hand on your leg while they're driving, or grips your arm in excitement. For so long, I'd wanted only to be alone, to sit each morning and evening in silence. Then suddenly, like a tsunami flooding in, taking everything away, I wanted to be always in company, to be touched by someone who loves me, at least one hand on me at all times. Don't let a door close between us.

Thinking back to the boy in the café, remembering being briefly held by him, it isn't the touch itself that made me feel polluted – it's that it was an act of love from someone I had just met, who used touch exploitatively. He cheapened love, like marrying sneakers, or lip gloss.

A hug that goes for longer than twenty seconds will cause your body to release oxytocin and lower your blood pressure. If a sales person touches my shoulder, apparently I'll like them more, I'll report a more positive experience. If I live in a country that tips, I'll tip higher to waiters who touch me. Researchers found Romanian orphans in understaffed orphanages, who were rarely touched, were half the weight and height they should be for their age and showed a raft of developmental disabilities. Parisian children who were touched often by their parents displayed less aggressive tendencies in a McDonald's playground than American children in a similar setting, who were touched less frequently. Why is it that when someone is upset we reach out to touch them? Who taught us this?

Look, I get it. Touch is good for us. But this thing, which is supposed to be beneficial, is also an act of violence. Surely the benefits of touch exist in an objective reality, outside the one we live in, in a world where no one ever hurt anyone, in which waiters are welcome to place their hands on us. But, in this reality, it can be hard to distinguish which touch is meant kindly when

214

we've been so socialised by dangerous touch. Surely the benefits balance each other out. While the physical act of touch might reduce cortisol, the social meaning of touch spikes it because many of us have been conditioned to be suspicious of touch. Why – seriously, why – would I want a waiter to touch me?

When I started working in a jewellery shop the person training me said, 'When you clip a bracelet on the customer, tap your fingers lightly on each side of their wrist. It builds intimacy.' This kind of touch that was being taught to me was gross. It was exploitative. I was using a form of love to improve my key performance indicators.

We're so easily moved. I can touch you and make you love me just a little bit more, and then I can use that love to gently part you from your money.

Perhaps violence is a different type of hurt to, say, a car crash, because it involves bodies touching. Perhaps that's what makes the idea of healthy social touch so confusing, because this thing that's meant to mean love, meant to mean intimacy, is so often an act of destruction against us.

I was thinking about this while absentmindedly watching a UFC fight. Near the end, the fighters rested their weight on each other. They paused the fight to hold each other like lovers. They rested this way, leaning into each other to take pressure off themselves, but also as protection. They can't be hit while their bodies are pressed together. What kind of arrangement is this?

Allow your enemy the same rest you take from them. Hold them close so they can't hurt you.

·

I'd planned a weekend trip to Melbourne with three male friends and as soon as we took our seats on the train I knew I'd made a terrible mistake. Later that night, I would pass out in our hotel room after drinking with all three of them. I'd wake up, the room spinning, with only one of them. After a horrible breakfast with this man, who was not only the first to assault me but also the first to kiss me, the first to do anything with me, we had an hour-long train ride, a short taxi ride to the naval base we were posted to, and a long walk back to the barracks. I'd barely spoken all morning and as soon as we reached the gates I sped up without saying goodbye and they let me get ahead of them. I finally got back to my room, and while blubbing and hiccuping, carefully placed my hand everywhere he'd touched me. I ran fingers through my hair, wrapped them around my arm, slid a hand up my own skirt. I understood something I didn't have a language for: that this was an important thing to do, though I couldn't explain why.

When I started dating again, none of my dates ever kissed me. I didn't want them to, even the ones I liked. But still, I wondered why no one tried. I wondered if I gave off a vibe, like a big 'fuck off' written on my forehead. I'd notice a hesitancy sometimes at the end of dates, like they were about to say something and then changed their minds. I wish the dating rules were more clearly delineated, like if there was a book we all had to read, and we could agree on things like 'the third date is the kiss date'.

On the second date with the man who is now my boyfriend, I wanted both to kiss him and not kiss him. As we approached my sister's house where I was staying, I was half listening to him, trying to decide which I wanted more: to be kissed now, or to wait. I knew my whole family was inside the house visiting for lunch and what if they came out? I'd also been aggressively chewing my lip and knew it would taste of blood. I still felt like it was too soon for this level of intimacy, even though we'd been texting every day for three weeks. I'd been spending evenings grinning at my phone like an idiot. If he'd known me better at this point, he'd have known I was overthinking this. I was doing what he calls 'getting up my butt': a multifaceted term that can mean becoming neurotic and obsessive, but can also mean thinking deeply and beautifully, unravelling the way things are, making good art. In whatever context we say it, the other knows exactly what we mean.

So we lingered outside my sister's house. I quickly calculated how long my family had been inside and if they were likely to be leaving soon. At the first sign of him tilting forward, I blurted out, 'My whole family is in there!' I was instantly relieved, disappointed, glad for an excuse, wishing I hadn't used it. He held my hand and laughed, and I wondered about taking the excuse back, while knowing that it was right, that though I felt so lucky, so full in my heart, I wasn't ready.

I know how this makes me sound. Like I think I'm so pure and holy that I can't be touched without a choir of angels in the background.

At church, a guest speaker decided everyone should hug the people around them. I slipped from my seat before anyone could try it and waited in the lobby till it was over. An older man saw me do this and came up to me after the service. 'You're a good girl,' he said. The implication was, I suppose, that I was keeping myself sacred. He meant well. He was a nice man. But I was uncomfortable for reasons I still can't work out. Perhaps we both felt in our bones that if touch is love, and love is intimacy, then this is a terrible, false thing to accept instead. But when he called me a good girl, I felt as I do when someone says I'm not like other girls and I want to answer, 'Is there something wrong with other girls?' Was he suggesting that the ones who stayed and walked about the room giving and receiving hugs are bad girls? That they're whoring themselves out for an approximation of love? This version of it that is candy-pink, chemical-sweet, fake and cheap? Others scolded me for leaving as the hugging started. 'Can't you just do it to be polite? Can't you just not be awkward?' I have heard this many times before. 'You make people uncomfortable.'

I don't want to be a good girl. I don't want to be a bad girl, or an awkward girl. I just want to decide who can touch me and when.

The following happens over and over: I meet someone for the first time, I hold my hand out to shake theirs. They say, 'No, sweetie, I'm a hugger.'

'Congratulations,' I want to say, 'but I'm a rape survivor.' I don't say this of course, so I allow myself to be enfolded against their body, and I remember another body, weighing me down. I remember things that make my brain shrink with shame, like a hot Townsville night when I was broken into. Or that boy in Melbourne moving my clenched fist down, down. Trauma is separate from both narrative and time, so there is a tired part of my brain that can't tell the difference between then and now, between that touch and this one.

I used to ask myself, what actually is it about rape that causes the harm it does, which has nothing to do with the physical pain of it? I used to ask myself, *Where does it hurt? Why does it hurt?*

This is what I've come up with. I think the thing about rape that hurts so much – and in a lesser way, the harm of unwanted touch – is the same thing that's at the heart of good sex, good touch. It isn't the physical act. It's the spiritual state of it. You allow someone inside your body with nothing between you and nothing to hide behind. You trust your partner. Good sex is good because it's awkward and messy and gross and sometimes painful, and that's OK with you and whoever you're with. But that position of vulnerability, in order to be exercised fully and rightly, must be given freely. Rape forces you into a position you should only be in with someone you've chosen. Rape doesn't just break into the body. The body can heal. Red blood cells rush to a wound and kiss it better. A nail breaks into the body if stepped on, but you don't carry the shape of that nail with you. Rape enters something else: something deeper than bones. It breaks into a safe place.

If the body houses something like a soul, then it also provides a bridge into it. Good sex crosses over that bridge and meets the soul, but so then does rape. How else can another body hurt me somewhere that my own body can't reach? I cannot enter in and pluck out the splinter that was left in me. Unwanted touch induces in me the same sick feeling, of an intimacy that isn't right, isn't real. It confuses love. I've had nightmares of being forced to marry someone I dislike, and in the dream, even the symbols of intimacy – the dress, the flowers, the person waiting at the end of an aisle – crawl under my skin. I could throw up, I could cut off parts of my body.

For this same reason, I can't read published diaries. A teacher suggested I read Flannery O'Connor's prayer diary, published after her death. Her eyes lit up when she talked about it and quoted from it. I went straight to the book shop. I saw it, almost gleaming, on the shelf, but as I reached out it was like it burned my fingers. I couldn't read this. I thought of my own prayer diary. How mournful and personal and pleading it was. How joyful and wild. How I'd written unchecked. Prayer can so often feel awkward as a voicemail, but writing prayer was like opening a great window in my chest. Those entries are so personal that even I can't read them back. How could I read something poured from another woman's heart without her consent?

When I heard Marilyn Monroe's diaries were read after her death, I had the strange feeling that I now recognise as being triggered. My limbs go heavy, my thoughts go silent, something in me falls backward out of my body. I could picture men in suits, bent over those small, sad books; running their hands over them, ripping out the pages, pushing them into the light, cold and exposed. One final violation.

Like good sex, a good and true diary should be uncensored, unembarrassed, and if given, given freely.

If the body is a bridge to something in me that's more than my body, that is my whole soul, then so – perhaps – is a diary. Red blood cells cannot heal a soul.

I've still not gotten to the heart of what I'm trying to say. All these words are only drawing a circle around the thing I mean. I've tried different words in different orders, and I can't seem to circle any closer. Maybe it's time to admit that words won't answer this question for me. This is not a problem that language can solve.

My abuser used to show up in everything I wrote, then I'd edit him out at the end, and each piece would have a him-sized hole in it, like I have a him-sized hole in me. He wrote to me on my birthday once. He said it had been a long time. He hoped I'd have a good one. 'Thank you,' I wrote back, and I shook like an earthquake for the rest of the day. All he ever did was touch me. It only took a moment.

It was almost six months into my new relationship that I finally started to believe I really was loved, that he wouldn't be put off me by some small thing. I stopped taking every silence, every less than enthusiastic response as proof, finally, that he was sick of my shit. It was only touch, specifically touch that was unsolicited, that could reassure me. When I took him to meet my sisters, I was convinced that he was over me, that we were over, and he was just waiting to tell me. I believed this until an hour or so in, when he reached under the table and gave my knee a light squeeze. I got no reassurance from the fact that he was putting himself through the most uncomfortable performance, enduring the difficult work of trying to impress a family. It was only that light touch that could make me feel OK.

He doesn't touch me when he sleeps. Early in our relationship, I tried not to be hurt by his back to me, his eye mask, his earbuds. He cocoons himself in sleep and I am not allowed in. One night, my wriggling kept him awake to the point where he had to roll out of bed and sleep on the floor. The next day he bought a mattress so firm and vast that he could sleep without being aware I was even there. On the old mattress, which sank in the middle, I'd been able to roll against him so maybe he'd remember me and reach out (he didn't).

One morning, he woke for a moment, rolled over to drape his arm across my waist, and fell back asleep. I'd been about to get up, but I stayed in bed, holding onto the arm, feeling that I'd never been happier. Never in my life. I thought about telling him this, but it would ruin it somehow. He might repeat the action simply to make me happy, and that too is an act of kindness; a different act of love, but not the love of waking for a moment and reaching out.

I hadn't known if I was in love with him yet. I'd been checking my body, assuming that's where love would be, somewhere I could reach with my hands. It wasn't there yet, not yet, and then suddenly yes, there it is. When he draped that arm across my waist I was surprised to find love is a quiet thing, at the end of worry. I was expecting a feeling of tipping backwards, but this was a stronger thing than falling. I had reached up through love. I had stood in love, like a pillar for him to lean on.

I hadn't yet told him I loved him, but when I moved past him in a tight space, I'd lay my hands lightly on his waist, and hope he knew what I meant. That I was trying to say I love you, that you're the most beautiful, the most, the most, the most.

I show him every essay he appears in, so he knows what I'm putting into the world. He was worried I'd made him sound like an arsehole for not touching me at night. He said, 'Can you explain that it's just because I have trouble sleeping? That I can't be constricted or distracted? It's not that I don't love you. It's just, you know, it's too hot.' Laughing, he pointed to the part where he laid his arm across my body. 'Sorry to tell you this, but I was probably checking whether you'd gotten up yet so I could stretch out.'

It made me wonder which small things I have done that made him feel loved, but which I didn't mean. And it's safe to misinterpret these actions, because we do love each other, even if it's not what we mean by that particular action. However, knowing it's only my interpretation that touch equals love doesn't make touch *feel* any different. What if that boy in the restaurant was just righting himself, what if someone knocked him as he passed me by? It makes no difference to my experience. All we have is our own perception, even when we know it's wrong. As we discussed this, he said, 'You've taken what you think when you're up your butt, and applied your interpretation to everyone else's intention. You got up everyone's butt.'

'I got up the world's butt.'

He laughed, and as he rolled off the bed he said, 'Yeah, you did. Write that.'

The willies

When I lived by the ocean I had nightmares of tsunamis; of waves coming through the windows; of the car filling with water as I tried to drive away. I'm afraid of fish, of icebergs, of underwater mountain ranges. I used to dream I was floating in space between huge cubes and circles, but when I reached out to grab a cube, I found it was small enough to fit in my hands and I was the huge object. I'd wake up crying, feeling that I couldn't get all the fear out of my body. When I was thirty, after remembering this dream for twenty-five years, I sat in a spa, mouth open, as a friend described having the exact same one. Another friend described the same thing but with sound, where a whisper was twice as loud as a scream. He said he felt sick thinking of it.

.

I'm not afraid of dying, but I'm afraid of heaven. Or, perhaps I'm afraid of the concept of forever. Maybe the fear that runs through all these things is size. Forever is too big, and I'm too small. It's the feeling of my little body next to an underwater mountain range. But forever is just a series of moments, and when I reach out it's small enough to fit in my hands.

.

I'm afraid of clusters of holes. Even the word 'cluster'. Even the word 'holes'. A florist near my house had a display of lotus pods in the window. When I walked past on the way to the bus, the holes in the lotus pod made me angry. I hated them so much. I wanted to smash my fist through the glass and burst through the window. I thought about how I'd kick the pots over, rip the plants out and break them on the remaining shards of glass. When the florist came rushing out of the back room, I'd throw the remains at her and say she was disgusting for thinking such a thing was beautiful, like displaying a tumour. 'Is this beautiful?' I'd yell, kicking it at her. 'Do you like them now?'

This is a fear I caught like a cold. A Buzzfeed journalist wrote about her phobia of holes, which she'd just discovered had a name. I scrolled through the pictures of strawberries, crumpets, a flesh-eaten face, and I thought, *She's right. I hate this too.* A friend held out her phone and showed me a photo of a diseased nipple, the skin burst in a cluster of small craters. She laughed and I wanted to take the phone and smash it on the ground.

·

I'm not afraid of dying, but I'm afraid of looking back at my life and not being satisfied, realising I've not been an active participant. When this fear takes hold, I have to run to the beach or plan a walk or a day trip. I sit shivering on the sand so I can feel that I'm filling my life with meaningful experiences.

·

My sister said she'd found a cool tree on a walk and wanted to show us. She led us through the bush in the obscene Queensland heat. The vines had entirely covered the old tree, taking its shape, and the tree had died inside, leaving a ghost behind, a hollow tree-shaped mass of vines.

I turned to my other sister, Jo, and found her leaning over her knees, a hand over her mouth, dry retching. Goosebumps had risen on her arms and the fine blonde hairs stood on end. She pointed to the vines without looking at it. 'That is disgusting. It's disgusting,' and she stormed off down the track, back the way we'd come.

If my fear is of size, Jo's is of one thing latching onto another, possessing and feeding off it. I've seen her react this way to barnacles on whales, and ultrasounds of babies in the womb.

I looked back to the vine structure, trying to imagine

her fear, and saw the vines as a leech, as a coloniser, a parasite. I was revolted that I'd touched it, like I'd petted a dead possum on the road.

·

I knew of someone who was so afraid of repetitive sounds that she had to sell her house when a family moved next door with a son who spent his evenings bouncing a basketball in the driveway.

·

I'm not afraid of dying, but perhaps I'm afraid of particular ways of dying, or the moment of realising I'm falling backwards out of this one life I got. I'm afraid of what comes next, but not death itself.

·

I'm not afraid of dying, but what I'm afraid of now, which I never feared before, is separation. Of what will happen to all this love when we're no longer here to take it from each other.

Ithaca

Our oldest stories are about love, about home. Maybe this is every story. We keep turning the same old coin, over and over, testing the different ways it catches the light.

When I think of Odysseus it isn't the famous scenes that stay with me: the Cyclops, the dog (oh, but the dog knew something of love). I think of Odysseus drifting in the sea, clinging to his raft off the coast of Phaeacia. You need to know where home is to know this is not the way. Sometimes I wonder: if I was in the same situation, lost on the ocean, would I finally know which way I wanted the current to take me?

.

I think we're at odds with love. It feels too heavy, like it could break our backs. I have loved to the point of distress. I've found myself wanting the love to leave my body so I can get on with my life. There's a reason people fainted in front of the Beatles. Love overwhelms.

Sometimes I'm afraid to grasp too tightly to joy, in case the thing I love is taken from me. Like resting against a door only to fall through a moment later.

.

Home is a bracelet strung with different beads. Home and love, home and food, home and things you can never return to. Home is a junction, and not a thing in itself. What might Odysseus' junction be? What beads were on his bracelet? Home and Penelope? Home and rocks? Home and role? Home is a thing to keep in your eye.

.

It's considered cool to love certain things; uncool to love others. It's cool to love film and music (some music), but not to love horses and *Warhammer*. And sometimes coolness depends not on what you love but how you love – how loudly and hysterically. It's one thing to love Harry Potter, but quite another to be found outside the cinema dressed as Hermione, a wand clutched in your hot little hand.

I've always loved the wrong things, and I've loved them too much. I knew every publicly available fact about the Spice Girls. I dreamed of being in the Baby-Sitters Club. I wanted diabetes like Stacey McGill because she made it seem so glamorous. I held aloft whatever thing I loved and stared at it with big wet eyes. I imbibed it into my personality. There's nothing elegant or composed about this type of love. There's a sweaty franticness to it; a breath-taking agony.

I've learned to regulate my enthusiasm, or at least to keep it covered over. I can shrug apathetically while quietly tempering the fireworks of obsession, red in the face with love. My life's work has been to pretend I'm not deeply, irredeemably uncool, while knowing that in an album somewhere is a photo of me dressed in the actual armour used in *Lord of the Rings*.

.

The thing with love is that it feels like rest. When I came out of lockdown and I couldn't stop the pace of my thoughts, couldn't slow my heartbeat, I knew I needed the kind of rest that I can only get from an obsession. I went back to the books I read as a teenager, His Dark Materials and Harry Potter. I wanted the kind of love that would take me out of myself, that would make me project all my thoughts onto something else. I wanted to give myself over to love. When a love like that embodies you, you aren't in your own mind. You're altering your state of consciousness. I used love as a remedy, as rest.

That kind of love is so pure. It has no material value. It can't be muddied by capitalism. It's a love of the thing itself, for love's sake. There's nothing material to be gained, only the way it makes you feel.

There's nothing like watching someone talk about the thing they love. I went on holiday with my partner David and his friends, who'd all bonded initially over their love for music. They've been in different bands together over the years. Music is the centrepoint of their community. I had no frame of reference for understanding their conversation, no way to participate. I don't know what a melody is. I can't distinguish which sound in a song is the drums. But to listen to them talk, to hear them exclaim when a note changes in a particular way, and see their analysis of a song swirling down to a level of detail accessible only by those truly in love. What a thing that was.

.

A friend moved into college accommodation, and her parents sold their house to travel around Australia in a campervan. 'I don't have a home anymore,' she told me, even though she hadn't been living in her parents' house when they sold it. When I questioned this, she said, 'My parents' house was still my home. Now I have nowhere to go. I feel displaced.'

I remember I had to sit down. The feeling I'd always had but never identified suddenly had a name; and it wasn't the way everyone felt; other people felt 'placed'.

There are houses my parents have moved in and out of so quickly I never even saw them. We describe eras not by years, but by which house we lived in. 'That was when we lived in Palm Beach.' 'That was during the Bonogin house.'

My friend said, 'If I was kidnapped, there's no one who would notice that I didn't come home. If you don't hear from me for a few days, can you try to find me?'

So maybe that's what a home is. Maybe it's someone waiting up for you, who'll notice if you're missing.

·

Maybe if Penelope had stopped waiting, if she'd shacked up with a suitor, Ithaca would be home to neither of them. Oh, but there was still the dog, the dog spent his life waiting.

·

I was starting to feel at home in Wellington. Starting to think maybe this is what it means to be placed. Then both my sisters decided they were leaving, and I felt myself drift above this place, realising that, if my family wasn't here, there was nothing to tether me. This is not a home. This is just a place I live.

·

I have laboured over this essay. I have stared at the screen and stared out the window at the ocean, and stared at my notes, and I've not figured it out. So I gave it up, and I went to the orchestra. We'd wondered why our seats were so cheap until we showed up and realised we were directly under the stage. I kept making awkward eye contact with the musicians. And then they started playing, and for two hours I listened with my thoughts racing, because this was love. You don't choose to play the oboe for a living unless you love it. Unless you're just especially good at it. (But can you be especially good at something if you don't love it?) We were all together in that vast high-ceilinged space because all these people love to make music. Love makes things happen.

Is it true to say you are what you love? Sometimes I think it's true. Other times, it seems like simplifying people down to their hobbies. But there's something to the idea. Perhaps it's that what you love, if you love it enough, affects the way you move through the world, the communities you join, the places you find connection, the way you think of yourself. And maybe there's something in how you love. If an oboe player travels far from the place she lives, and meets another oboe player, has she found a small sort of home? If she, like Odysseus, found herself drifting in the ocean, would she kick the raft in the direction of her oboe?

.

Love means we don't chew grass in fields or eat nutrition blocks. It's why we have things that are beautiful and make no money. Love leads to innovation. We don't just survive. We delight, we have joy. So in that way, love is who we are. Is this how we're most like God? Is this what it means to be made in his image? Not that we look like God, but that we love; that we make things.

In whose image was Odysseus made? His gods didn't love anyone.

·

If home is love, can you have a home and yet be lonely? If you're lonely, are you in some way away from home?

·

James Corden posted a video in which Paul McCartney showed him around his home town. At the end of the video, McCartney, with a small band, hides behind a curtain in a quiet pub. When someone picks a song from a jukebox, the curtain pulls back and McCartney starts to sing. People rush in from the street, Corden dances with a woman behind the bar. A young woman shouts for the camera's attention, and points excitedly to the Beatles tattoo on her forearm. By the end of the set, the pub is packed. McCartney ends by inviting Corden onto the stage, and starts to sing the first lines of 'Hey Jude'. The same young woman jumps up and down and then covers her mouth, bursting into tears. The crowd settles now. They move slowly, singing along. And I thought,

This is what art can do. I want to make something that does that.

No, this is what love can do.

.

We were learning how to weave together a pepeha in a te reo course, and a man named Colin kept saying, 'I don't have a mountain. The one I'm using isn't really mine. It's so far away from me.' He couldn't get through his mihi without reminding us that the mountain he was using was not really his. One week the woman next to me sighed and said, 'Someone give Colin a mountain.'

I don't have a mountain either, no awa, no connection to the crowd of ancestors standing behind me. I just picked the one I lived on. Unlike Colin, I did this quietly. But as I repeated every week in class that this mountain was mine, I felt it shift into my bones, so like the bones of my ancestors I wouldn't recognise, which are buried near that same mountain.

Because the *Telegony*, the final poem in the Epic Cycle, is lost, it's easy to forget the thing about Odysseus, the thing that says everything about him: that he leaves again. After all that.

Some are meant to have a home yet always be far from it.

A few weeks after the te reo course finished, my love asked if I'd leave Wellington and move to a new city with him, and I knew two things at once: that this is my home, and that I can leave it.

To the holy place

Once last winter when we were mapping out the pilgrimage on his kitchen table, he said to me, 'Well, what are you afraid of, then?' I said nothing. 'Nothing.' —Anne Carson

I must have read about the Camino somewhere. I've tried to remember where but it was too long ago, and since then I've read about it everywhere, everywhere I could. I couldn't tell you why it grabbed hold of me because I don't even like hiking. Maybe it was the idea of doing something old, something that's mentioned in Chaucer. Maybe it's just to do something difficult. I mentioned it in passing to David, that it was something I'd always wanted to do. I mentioned it the fourth time we hung out, when I asked 'What do you want?' and heard him give my own answer: 'To be free.' Six months later we thought maybe we'd find that freedom in a house in the South Island. We said to each other, 'Don't get your hopes up yet. It might not happen,' but we chose which coffee machine we'd buy and which prints we'd put on our walls. We sent each other screenshots of furniture, and real estate listings, always careful to say, 'just hypothetically'.

In a moment, in a decision someone else made, the plan fell over, and we realised we hadn't really believed it was hypothetical. We'd got our hopes all the way up, and here we were in the same place, very much not free. We watched TV and got depression meals delivered, until David said, 'What was that walk you wanted to do?' and by the end of the weekend, we had a new plan. We couldn't exist without one.

On weekends we haul ourselves up every mountain in the Hutt Valley, and along the river. Sometimes we walk the 30 kilometres from David's house to mine, stay the night, then walk back the next day. We discover the wonder of walking poles, properly fitted packs, and merino everything. All our money goes into a savings account or is blown at Macpac. He's been reading forums about what to pack and what boots to buy. I've been reading Anne Carson. He says poetry won't get me over the Pyrenees. I say he doesn't know poetry.

Every story I read except for Carson's is of someone finding themselves, or having a cool mystical time. I read *Kinds of Water* because it doesn't seem like she's even enjoying herself. We're not going on a pilgrimage, we're going on an 800-kilometre walk. We have nothing to find except a way to be free.

I have to remove my presence from so many places: David's house, the house I'm selling, the house I've been staying in. Despite ruthlessly throwing out and giving away my possessions, everywhere I turn there are more things. More tiny bottles of moisturisers and vitamins, endless bobby pins, mascaras and eyeshadows. I am shedding constantly, and not just possessions, but bits of thread, pebbles tracked in on my shoes, and hair – hair everywhere, on every surface. I want to be away from all signs that I have occupied a space. On the road I will only be walking away from myself and whatever I leave is left behind me. I will get cleaner and cleaner as I go.

Finally, three houses' worth of stuff gone, we walk out the door with only a pack each and David's mum drives us to the airport.

We have three days in Paris to acclimatise before starting the Camino. It's supposed to be a time to rest but there's so much to see in Paris when you're simps for a nice building. Plus our flat is so small that neither of us can stand up straight, so we run around all day and return too exhausted to even watch a movie. Tourism is so strange – you just walk to places and look at things. We're filling our eyes up. In the morning I wait for David to wake so we can get espresso and pastries and I can tell him everything I just read about flying buttresses.

Everything tastes better in France, but the food

is so rich and nothing has vegetables in it. I've been uncomfortably full for days. We go on a hunt for clementines to keep scurvy at bay and marvel that everyone is having dinner at our bedtime.

The last night in Paris I wake with that tight throat feeling that comes before a cold. We start tomorrow with a 20-kilometre hike and it will probably rain. Our accommodation is booked along the trail for the first week and if we delay by even one day we'll have to cancel and rebook everything. The Covid test is negative so I tell David, 'I'll be all right. It's just a cold.'

We catch a train to San Sebastian where we'll begin on the Northern Route as it's the most scenic and quieter than the more popular French Route. The architecture changes as we get closer to Spain, roof tiles curving. Bright fields of rapeseed whizz past. Everyone else was smart and brought snacks but I'd been caught out by my romantic idea of a bar carriage. I stumble through the train expecting to find something glamorous and clinking, with wait staff and a shining bar. The reality is less Oriental Express and more like exactly how you'd imagine train food. I present David with stale chicken sandwiches, clammy muffins and, inexplicably, a free jar of apple sauce.

.

We purchase blood oranges and eat them very fast. It is already late when you wake up inside a question. Rose petals are being swept from the church steps as we pass, and faces in the doorway are lit with vague regret. Someone has roused the town. . .

In San Sebastian we get things ready for the next morning: walking poles to the correct height, clothes laid out, bags packed and repacked to be more efficient. David shaves his entire face and head for efficiency. He thinks it will make him more aerodynamic. My cold seems to be better already.

I wake up in the dark, soaked in sweat, sheets drenched. I sleep on top of the duvet and in the morning that's wet too. My nose is completely blocked and my stomach hurts, but we've come all this way. We can't use up our days off before we've even started. As we walk along the beach towards the trail, I load myself with drugs and nose spray while David films the scenery. People passing call out 'Buen Camino' and David shouts it back. 'You realise that means "Good Camino",' I say. He knows this but hadn't realised it makes no sense to say it back to someone just going to work. But we're stuck for a response, between languages. I accidentally say 'bonjour' each time, which is the only word that comes to me when I'm outside an English-speaking country. David says variants of, 'Buen ca – ah shit – ci. I mean gracias,' by which time the speaker is gone.

The trail begins with a steep path over a mountain

and I want to feel victorious. We're here. After all that planning and training, and beyond that even. Since whatever it was that sparked the desire to do this, so many years ago. I'm trying now to remember what I'd imagined it would be like and what the spark felt like, what desire felt like, but I can't bring it up. I can't conjure a single reason why I'd thought this would be a good idea. I can hardly breathe and I'm already running out of tissues. The cold and the movement are making my nose drip constantly and I shove my nostrils full of tissues so I don't have to keep sniffling. The trail is marked with yellow arrows that David keeps track of while I trudge behind, disappointed in myself, wishing I could remember what it was like not to be climbing this mountain so I'd remember what it was like to want to. A French man, also doing the Camino, stops us and points in the opposite direction. We take several minutes and various translation devices to establish that we were actually going the right way. Without a common language, we find ourselves saying 'Ayyy' and laughing, throwing our hands out, all too loud and too outgoing. I laugh at jokes I don't understand and realise how incapable I am of understanding non-verbal communication.

We've been walking an hour when the cold and flu pills kick in. Suddenly my body seems to open up again. I can breathe through my nose. My stomach unclenches. We stop to look at a patch of moss that inhales and sighs with the spring underneath it and I feel taken over by a feeling of bliss; to be in this place with this person, to have no job and a bit of money, to stop and eat some fruit with a view all the way to the ocean.

But soon I feel drowsy and when I translate the Spanish on the box of pills I realise they're for nighttime. I've never felt my eyes drift closed on a hike before. I could lay my head on the soft grass and fall asleep right here.

David spends entire days in a state of bliss, even when the mountains never end, and when I stop replying to his happy chatter because I'm grumpy and just trying to breathe. At the end of each day I apologise for being terrible company.

On the third day I'm no better. A sign tells us we're three kilometres from our destination point, but after an hour of walking another sign tells us we're still three kilometres away. This happens twice. We're already four kilometres over the distance we expected to walk today and I want to chuck my bag off the cliff and throw a tantrum like you've never seen. But I keep walking. I always keep walking, and for the last 500 metres we walk through a green valley along a stream that looks like it's from a fantasy novel. A perfect pastoral scene. It's so beautiful and I don't want a bar of it. I don't care about beauty or walking or how many thousands of years old this path is. I want to be in our hotel watching *Call My Agent* on David's phone like we do every evening, hoping that tomorrow my cold will be better, and gearing myself up to do it all over again every day for thirty-three days.

What makes a pilgrimage different to a long walk? Should something happen? I've barely thought about God, even though that's what this road is for. I don't think about anything. Not a thought in my head. My mind gets stuck on a loop track. I sing 'Royals' over and over all day like a piece of shit.

So many people asked if I was doing this as a faith walk. I said no and I meant it. But maybe, maybe I did expect something to happen. Maybe that's what the desire to do the Camino was, to see what would happen. How does a pilgrim know when she's become one?

.

Pilgrims were people who figured things out as they walked. On the road you can think forward, you can think back, you can make a list to remember to tell those at home.

That evening I wash my clothes in the sink and go for a coffee in the hotel to give David some time alone without me whinging and sniffling. When he comes down for dinner we put menu items into Google Translate and order something that translates to 'head on a grill'. The fish that arrives turns out to be the best meal of my life. We drink an enormous bottle of local cider and share a Basque cheesecake looking out over the valley that stretches all the way to the ocean.

I ask David what he thinks about as he walks. He says he makes a list of what we have to do to be ready for tomorrow, he looks out for the yellow arrows, and he takes everything in and lets it fill him up with joy and a sense of pride in how hard we worked to get here, and how we're here and we're free. I ask if he thinks about God. He says no, then yes, then, 'I think about how amazing it is that all this exists, and how I walked past this thing that's been here for a hundred years and will be here for another hundred years, and I'm simply passing it like a passenger on a train.'

Like every night I wake having sweated through all the sheets. In the morning, I allow myself one tear, just one, and then I'm ready to go again.

Did I bring a question here? I think I did, but I don't know what it is. The only thing I've learned isn't about God or penance. It's only about myself: that I can keep going. That I can just keep going forever and forever, one foot down and then the other.

When I'm still sick on the fourth day David asks if I want a rest, but we're in a town with one bar and no restaurant. All we could find for dinner was a single tortilla to share. If we stop now it'll mess up our booked accommodation for the next few nights, so I tell him not to worry, but in the morning my breath whistles inside me. It howls and wheezes. I can feel cords of phlegm down my throat. I try to cough quietly in the bathroom so as not to wake him, but I'm seized by it. It bends my body over. When I shuffle back to bed David has woken up and says, 'We're not going any further.' I sleep in while he cancels three days' worth of hotels and books us a new hotel in the nearest decent-sized town. We spend an entire day's budget on a taxi to get us there. By the end of the day, he's sick too.

.

'I do not wish to sound Sokratic' – between angry bites of *tortilla* – *'but what is your definition of penance?'*

Our hotel is a palatial 600-year-old building. The owner dresses head to toe in All Blacks gear and gives David his full family history, showing him the walls lined with old photos, while I sit over an espresso and try to look healthy and awake. As soon as we can, we block out all light in our room, get the aircon going, and then collapse into the enormous bed.

For the next few days, we lie in the dark, swamped in blankets, our heads bent over Netflix on David's phone screen. At night we stumble into clothes and try to look like humans in the fancy-as-shit hotel restaurant. We eat grilled octopus and salmon tartare while mouth breathing, eyes half closed. For the second time, one of us takes too many cold and flu pills. This time it's David. He stumbles on the stairs into the restaurant and is so drugged he can barely see me, head lolling on the other side of the table. Two minutes after dinner we're back in undies, starfished on the bed.

With our budget in ruins and our nasal passages working again, we decide to join the French Route. The Camino is meant to be crowded but we've barely seen anybody on the Northern Route, and have only spoken to one other person aside from each other.

When we arrive in Santo Domingo, we're surrounded by pilgrims and, after having wanted to speak to people, we avoid them. We feel like fakers because we walked a few days, spent a week in a lush hotel, and then jumped ahead so as not to get behind.

The night before we begin I feel pre-hike nerves because it's been so long. Once again I find myself worrying that I won't enjoy it, that it will be too hot or too hard. But in the morning we find ourselves walking in a line of other pilgrims, past acres and acres of rapeseed stretching in a patchwork to the horizon, and finally *this* feels like the Camino.

On the French Route locals set up portable cafés and breakfast spots along the trail, so for the first time we find ourselves in a crowd. Over coffee and pastry, we watch as a school trip pulls up and teenagers wearing shells set off running down the trail. Off to the side a man does a sort of merengue with two girls, and afterwards grabs his staff, which looks like something out of *Lord of the Rings*. It surely must be too heavy to be useful, but off he trots, staff swinging, plucking an ear of wheat and tucking it into his fedora. An Australian girl is sitting with her toe-shoe-wearing companion and we hear them greet every pilgrim like an old friend. This feels like the first day of school where everyone already knows each other. Most of these people have been walking together for two weeks already.

The day goes so fast. Down the road I chat with the Australian, Alison, who has left Toe Shoes Girl sitting in the shade, shoes off, rubbing her feet.

In our hostel, people discuss whether they'll skip the Meseta. It's 180 kilometres of near featureless plains with little shade, nothing to look at, no cafés in small villages. The Meseta is a few days away but we've had to skip so much. Only us and one other person are doing it. A few hours later, all the people we just met are standing around in their underwear. David walks into the tiny shower and comes face to face with a used sanitary pad. In a room of thirty other people snoring, we barely sleep, and in the morning I wake with bed bug bites and say, 'Hey, we wanted an adventure.'

We've now been travelling for nearly three weeks and we've not met a single New Zealander. I keep stopping Australians, thinking I hear a Kiwi accent, but I've been wrong every time. Where is everyone? We run into Alison every few days, and David can never remember her name even though it's literally the same as mine. We see Toe Shoes Girl limping along, sometimes with Alison, but often sitting by the road. Occasionally we see Fedora Boy striding ahead. He has more wheat in his hat now and I wonder how it doesn't fall in his face and make him sneeze. Nearly everyone we pass on the road makes a joke about David's height and we laugh like it's the first time we've heard it.

We learn that walking is the easiest part. It's usually done by midday. The real work is finding accommodation, washing clothes in the sink, washing yourself, finding lunch, seeing the town, trying to stay awake, finding dinner, hoping the clothes will dry. We do our little tasks with aching knees and feet. We groan into standing positions like old men. My calf muscles spasm, and each cold morning we haul our packs onto our shoulders and set off, stopping at the first village for breakfast.

A Canadian pilgrim we met yesterday points us out to a cyclist but he's too far away to understand why. An hour later, the cyclist whizzes past and in our own accent yells, 'Kia ora my Kiwi friends', and this is better than food and water. This is better than stopping in a village for a coffee and a pastry. I can do another 10 kilometres on this. An army marches on familiar things from home.

.

Ahead of me walks a man who knows the things I want to know about bread, about God, about lovers' conversations . . .

So, Anne, you want to know about conversations between lovers, as if all we do is whisper to each other, heads on pillows. I'll tell you what lovers talk about: muesli bars, whether the socks will dry in time, what presents to buy our mums, the weather forecast for tomorrow, or we don't talk at all. This is an intimacy I've never reached before. I have talked and talked and talked until they went away and I could sit in silence once more. Now, words die in my mouth because I don't need to say anything. Your Cid and mine walk with a star in their shoe, smiling all the way down the road. You and I walk behind, staring at their backs for hours a day. Your Cid asks you about penance. I'm the one who brings that up. We remind ourselves that it's not what we're here to do. We're just here to walk.

There's buzz among the walkers because those who've phoned ahead haven't been able to get accommodation in any of the towns before Burgos, so most are racing ahead to get the last rooms in hostels. A German man we met a few days ago strides past. He started Camino spontaneously, bringing only chino shorts and a pair of jeans. He'd stood next to me brushing his teeth in only tight blue briefs while I kept my eyes on the ceiling.

As he passes us he shouts, 'I'm walking all the way to Burgos!' a grin on his face.

'It's 50 kilometres away,' I remind him.

'I know!' but he's gone, racing ahead, and we never see him again.

We give up on finding anywhere to stay and after 30 kilometres, decide to jump ahead a leg and catch a taxi to

Burgos, agreeing not to tell anyone that we're checking into a nice hotel and ordering Uber Eats. We remind each other again, we aren't doing penance. Tomorrow is the beginning of the Meseta.

I lie awake, nervous about the miles of nothing that wait for us after Burgos.

If I'd done this walk a few years ago there would be no fear in a plain stretch of road. There would be no unsafe place. But now, there is a hot centre in my mind, a void I try to skip my thoughts over. A place where God is and everything I think he used to be and might be now. I try not to think of being a child afraid of the rapture, of hell, of drugs and swearing. Or being in my twenties and so filled with the uncomplicated joy of thinking I understood things, of how simple everything can be when you're so sure of the rules. What if tomorrow I remember the time I thought if I got really into this game of Uno I could forget everything I was afraid of, and the memories wouldn't return to me after the game was over. What if I remember peeling apples thinking *If I don't break the skin it means I'm not going to hell*. If I remember these things with only road in front of me there won't be anything to distract me, nothing else to think about, and I'll get pulled into that hot centre. And of course I'm now thinking of these things, yet here I am, walking 800 kilometres to a church wondering if this is love, because God should have been so easy to let go of.

Maybe this is the question I brought, hoping for some great lesson. It does feel better though, more honest, to not know anything.

.

Look again at the photograph. Two figures moving on the Meseta, running slowly on a table of gold. Running with arms out, mouths open.

We have to hold back from stopping too often on the Meseta to take photos. For hours we walk past fields of wheat, susurrating in the breeze. We get caught in a storm which blows us along the road, hunched against it. The few villages we walk through have Bible verses and Biblical scenes painted on every wall. There is nothing on the horizon except more fields, splattered with poppies like blood stains. It helps not to think about the end of the day. There is no forward or back. There is only this foot after that one, poles hitting the ground. A horizon that never moves, never gets closer. We are walking on the spot.

I've never been able to meditate. There is only forward and back for me. The present moment is only a hinge. It contains nothing but breath, and I can't linger on something empty. What else is there to think about but forward and back?

But here, it's forward and back that's empty. Neither exists. We don't move. There is only this breath, then this one, then this one.

Our hostel is a green paradise in the desert. Our knees ache from walking on a flat terrain for several days. We limp through the paradise and I lie on the grass. At dinner we sit next to a Canadian woman named Kay who has a quiet contentment about her. We talk about how we settle ourselves each day and make a home for a night. Each pilgrim has a different routine. David pulls his clothes bag and toiletries out of his pack and lines them up as soon as he gets in, ready to be used and packed back in the next morning. He does this before he even sits down. 'After that, I'm settled.' Kay has a small alarm clock that she arranges; then she sends a single photo to her partner, wraps her sore feet, and she's done. 'A ritual for home,' she says. We make small homes wherever we go. I don't have a ritual. I drop my bag down and myself beside it. A week before we left Aotearoa my Dad asked me where I feel my home is and I said, 'David'.

.

What do you find there? That is a good question. Who would you be if you knew the answer?

We run into Alison on the way to Mansilla. She's waving goodbye to Toe Shoes Girl, who squeezes past the café owner on the way out the door. The man pats Toe Shoe Girl's arm and she whips her head around, and yells, 'Don't touch me.' She jogs in her toe shoes to catch up with Fedora Boy, now with so much wheat in the brim of his hat that you can barely make it out.

Alison tells us they're now walking together and sleeping outside under the stars. She says Toe Shoes Girl is walking 40 kilometres a day, despite the pain in her feet, because she wants to keep up with him.

'He won't wait for her?'

Alison shrugs. She seems annoyed and we get the feeling more has passed between them. We discuss our plans for the day, how far we're walking. We've chosen our next accommodation because it has a pool, even though the host added me on WhatsApp and texts constantly.

The café owner says 'Buen Camino' as we leave, and we say it back. We never did get that right.

Back on the road I say to David, 'Poor Toe Shoes Girl. Fedora Boy is never going to text her back.'

The thought of the pool sustains us through the 33-degree heat. When we arrive, the pool is not exactly what it looked like in the photos. It's an inflatable above-ground pool with a wobbly A-frame ladder that we have to drag over ourselves. There's a film of bugs and pollen on the surface of the water. The owner pops up constantly like a Spanish Basil Fawlty, checking in, reminding us that if we wish to use the fan in our room it will cost extra. The pool ladder shakes as I carefully climb over. It shakes even more violently as David climbs and I'm just about to warn him but it's too late. He places his foot on the inflatable edge of the pool rather than the top of the ladder and his body slides back down the other side, disappearing from view. I pop my head over the edge and see all six-foot-six of him sprawled on the pavement. A woman sunbathing under the fruit trees takes her sunglasses off and glares at us for having laughed too loud and roused her from her slumber.

David landed on his heels first and it only hurts a little, so we send the story to our family chats. We laugh and laugh until David says, 'Do my feet look swollen?' soon both feet are puffy to the ankles, the skin stretched and purple, and he can barely walk. Things happen in instants. All of life is one instant after another and suddenly you are walking in a different direction, turning the map to see where you are.

·

We cross the top of the world and descend into the city of León in conditions much different than expected.

The next morning we catch a taxi to León where we'd planned a two-day break to explore the city, but David can hardly walk to the café across the road for breakfast, so I go exploring without him. It's a different country alone. Without David by my side, a man calls out to me from a bar, and someone follows me down the street speaking Spanish while I pretend to be busy on my phone. How long has it been since I did anything by myself? I bring him back photos of old buildings, and a punnet of strawberries.

The swelling gets worse. He still can't walk and we're supposed to be back on the trail tomorrow. We find an apartment to stay in for another few days and I do grocery shopping and cooking, and yell at David every time he tries to walk. But there's nothing for it. His feet still ache, and are twice their usual size. I don't know if I should say it out loud, but I wonder if this journey is over. We've spent more time recovering from things than we have walking. In the end, he says it.

'You could go on alone?'

'I don't want to go without you.'

I visit the cathedral, leaving him with his feet up, eating chips and watching Formula 1 and I have to laugh. This is not the typical posture of a pilgrim.

.

Stars are spitting out of the cathedral as we enter Compostela: the cathedral! No it is not a mirage, this stupendous humming hulk of gold . . .

I sit in the cathedral in the light from the stained glass window and get Anne Carson's essay out on my phone, scrolling to the end: the arrival in Compostela. I know that if we don't finish now, we'll never come back, no matter what we tell ourselves. Maybe I could go on alone. There are twelve days left. All the accommodation is booked. Have I even enjoyed myself so far? That's not the right question, but, having asked myself this whole time why I'd wanted to do it, here I am, with the journey possibly over, wanting it again. I want to finish, though I still couldn't tell you why. Maybe what I want is just to walk triumphant into Compostela. Maybe I only want to have done it, not actually to do it. I want it behind me, not in front. We trained so much for this, we walked so many Wellington hills. Perhaps we should have spent more time getting in and out of swimming pools.

I know that if I go alone I won't have a good time. I'll cry in hostels, I'll want to talk to people but be too awkward to start conversations. All the way I'll be thinking of David relaxing in a hotel somewhere and I'll wonder again why I've done this. Every footstep will sound like 'why, why, why'.

But maybe I should always have done this alone. It's too easy to let David look out for the yellow arrows and book the accommodation while I trudge behind him, like I used to follow my mum around the supermarket, my mind emptying, thoughts going flat when I'm with someone who can look after things, look after me. Maybe I want to look after myself again like I did for years before David came along. Maybe I want, once more, to be strong and brave. The desire to finish is bone-deep, like it used to be.

I want to crawl under the pews and cry, though I'm not sure why. We don't know what will happen yet. Nothing is decided, but I know if I have to, I'll go alone.

Of course, by the time I get back to our apartment, I've realised we can't afford separate accommodation for each of us, and David will need help. He can't get to the supermarket alone or get down the stairs to pick up Uber Eats. Despite what I decided in a lit-up cathedral, we have to do this together or not at all.

The insurance company tells us to go to the hospital where we chat to other injured pilgrims, and a tiny nurse pushes David around in a wheelchair, even though he's taller than her while sitting down. He has tendon and muscle damage all the way up his legs and needs to rest. They think he should be better in a week or so. But 'better' doesn't mean 'immediately walk 100 kilometres', so we go out for coffee and we make a decision. It's over. Instead of finishing the Camino, we rent a car and drive to Barcelona where we can stay in one place for a month.

In Barcelona, we say what a luxury it is to buy a bottle of milk and know we'll be in one place long enough to drink it. David goes to physio every week but recovery is slow. We ride bikes around the city until he can walk comfortably again.

.

I have come through countries, centuries of difficult sleep and hard riding and still I do not know the sense of things when I see it, when I stand with the pieces in my hands.

The apartment block opposite ours has wide glass doors into every living room. The building is like a doll's house cracked open. We have a cross-section view of people going about their lives, and we watch them from our small porch while we hang the washing out. A woman dyes her daughter's hair while the girl sits at a computer. A couple watch TV, his head in her lap. A woman lies on the couch and spends an entire day scrolling through her phone. From our own living room we hear a shuffling, scraping sound and make a bet as to what it is – the loser has to make dinner. On the deck when we've placed our bets, we see a man in the ground floor apartment cleaning his freezer, scraping a spatula over the ice. David's guess was right. It's enraging when he's right, but I get dinner on.

Something has shifted. I have in myself a kind of shelter. I can go out on my own, I can stay home while David goes to physio without checking my clock, wondering how far away he is and pacing the flat. I'm starting to see that in deciding I could get to Compostela alone, in realising I'd be able to do it, I finished something. I did what I came here to do. A horrible thought occurs to me that makes all my insides cringe. What if sitting in that cathedral – the wrong cathedral – I really did find myself. God, that is so embarrassing.

On our last night in Barcelona it starts to rain. The last time we saw rain was on the Meseta when we dove for raincoats and raced to cover ourselves and our bags. This time, everyone comes out of their homes to watch: the daughter with the dyed hair, the man with the clean fridge, the couple. All with heads tilted, watching the sky, watching each other, until, one by one, we drift back inside with rain on our faces.

Every pilgrim hits the mark in his own way.

Acknowledgements

My first thanks to the many patient friends who read *The New Jerusalem* over and over in its multiple forms, as it passed from short story to novel to memoir to essay. Be grateful you missed the high school drama play.

Thanks also to the wonderful writing teachers I've been blessed to learn from over the years: Chris Price, Jessie Hennen, Elizabeth Knox, and particularly William Brandt who suggested as an experiment I write something that really happened, and Harry Ricketts who taught me you don't *have* to write short stories. What a gift, to be taught by such gentle geniuses. Acknowledgement should also go to Terese Svoboda who made half the class cry, but inspired 'Have you ever seen the rain'. My workshop companions in those classes also count as teachers in their own right. Particularly my MA cohort: Madison Hamill, Rose Lu, Anna Rankin, Tim Grgec, Glenda Lewis, Susanne Jungersen, Catherine Russ, and Charlotte Forrester. And you too, Jake, who gave me the concept of words having a mouthfeel, which I'm never not thinking about.

Tracey Schuyt and Caoimhe McKeogh: support group, teen detectives, and occasional paparazzi. I couldn't have done it without you and I wouldn't have wanted to. And thanks to Caffe Mode who let the three of us sit there for entire days.

Thanks to my parents for impulsively moving us to Ethiopia at the end of a civil war, giving me plenty to write about. Also for teaching me to value stories, and for agreeing not to read this one.

Thanks to Hilary, Brian, Kārena, and all the Coffeys for welcoming me into your family, but also for letting me commandeer an office in your house, and introducing me to New World pizza.

Thanks also to Tom and Jill for being my first supporters, when my writing consisted of café reviews and embarrassing Tumblr poems.

When I started writing this I hadn't met David, yet I finished it sitting across from him, his cat asleep on my notes, the dog in the corner chewing through my new Birkenstock. Much of this book has come from our conversations, our walks around the block, and our adventures. It would be a very different story if not for David and the life we're building. It would also have a different ending if he were better at climbing into swimming pools. Thanks for letting me write about you, right from date 1. Also for making me laugh, helping me with technology, planning our trips, and for being a home wherever we go. Buttloads of love.